THE ROUGH GUIDE TO
The PlayStation Portable

D1022460

ROUGH
GUIDES

www.roughguides.com

Credits

The Rough Guide to the PlayStation Portable

Edited by Kate Berens
Cover, text design & layout:
Cathleen Elliott, flyleaf design LLC
Proofreading: Lisa Grzan
Screen recreations: David Ardito
Production: Aimee Hampson

Rough Guides Reference
Series editor: Mark Ellingham
Editors: Peter Buckley, Duncan Clark,
Tracy Hopkins, Sean Mahoney,
Matthew Milton, Joe Staines, Ruth Tidball
Director: Andrew Lockett

Publishing Information

This first edition published September 2006 by
Rough Guides Ltd, 80 Strand, London WC2R 0RL
345 Hudson St, 4th Floor, New York 10014, USA
Email: mail@roughguides.com

Distributed by the Penguin Group
Penguin Books Ltd, 80 Strand, London WC2R 0RL
Penguin Putnam, Inc., 375 Hudson Street, NY 10014, USA
Penguin Group (Australia), 250 Camberwell Road, Camberwell, Victoria 3124, Australia
Penguin Books Canada Ltd, 10 Alcorn Avenue, Toronto, Ontario, Canada M4V 1E4
Penguin Group (New Zealand), Cnr Rosedale and Airborne Roads, Albany, Auckland, New Zealand

Printed in Italy by LegoPrint S.p.A.

Typeset in Minion, Nobel and Trade Gothic.

A catalogue record for this book is available from the British Library

ISBN 13: 978-1-84353-754-0
ISBN 10: 1-84353-754-0

1 3 5 7 9 8 6 4 2

THE ROUGH GUIDE TO

The **PlayStation Portable**

written by

Nicholas Gilewicz & Sean Mahoney

ROUGH
GUIDES

www.roughguides.com

Contents

NETWORKING

FIRMWARE, SOFTWARE & HOMEBREW

EXTRAS

FIRST AID

RESOURCES

Introduction

Why a book about the PSP?

What is there to say about a portable video game system? A lot, as it turns out. Before the dot-com stock crash of 2000, computer and media companies were burning through their venture capital while promising us the Holy Grail of convergence: music, pictures, radio, films, and TV would all be digital, and portable enough to carry around in our pockets. Many of those companies are now long gone (some consumed by a behemoth competitor), but convergence has shown up alive and well in the form of the PlayStation Portable.

The PSP is the closest thing to a truly convergent media device available today, and adds WiFi Internet connectivity to boot. Besides playing the most sophisticated hand-held games we've seen, with it you can surf the Web, listen to your iTunes music library, watch and download movies, wirelessly interact with other PSPs, and run freeware homebrew programs that provide all sorts of other high-tech functionality. Did you know that you can play old Nintendo games on the PSP? Or that you can turn it into a universal remote control?

Part of the purpose of this book is to show, step-by-step, how to make the most of your PSP's basic capabilities. But another purpose is to explore how the PSP really does bring together all sorts of digital content, and to carefully guide you through the sometimes complicated integration of your media files with the PSP's Memory Stick. We also include an extensive selection of PSP accessories to help you personalize your PSP. And for those of you inclined to tinker under the hood, we explore a few advanced procedures that you're sure to find a worthy challenge.

The PSP isn't just about playing Grand Theft Auto: Liberty City Stories or watching the latest Hollywood blockbuster. The PSP is changing our relationship with digital media in ways that were promised to us years ago, but that we're just now beginning to see. Read on to find out how.

Acknowledgements

The authors would like to thank both Nadine Kavanaugh and June Kim for their support throughout the writing of this book, and especially for turning a blind-eye while we played videogames and called it research. We'd also like to give a big thanks to Kate Berens at Rough Guides. Her keen editorial eye coupled with her experience as a videogamer have made this book better than we could have possibly imagined.

For image support, we'd like to thank Ruth Speakman of Sony Europe, Kimberly Otzman of Sony America, Eric Yeung at Team X-tender, Neo at Neoflash, Robert Kao at Naki World, Michael Kirkham at Spectravideo, Lawrence from the Brando Workshop, Clement Wen at Bluetake, Marc Richards at Arkon Resources, Keri Barnes and Mari Hersh at Vector Products, Heather Leech at Gamexpert, Ryan from DecalGirl, and Chad & Paco Allen for their NYC 2123 artwork.

BASICS &
BUYING

△
□
○
✕

01

What is the PSP?

what it's for and what else it can do

You already know that the PSP is designed to play games and movies you buy at the store, but it's also capable of much, much more. This book will show you just what's possible with the PSP, how to fully exploit its capabilities and capacity, what its strengths and weaknesses are, and how to use them or get around them. You'll learn all sorts of techniques later in the book, but in order to get there, we need to start at the beginning.

THE BASICS

The PSP is essentially what its initials stand for – the PlayStation Portable. Just as Sony's PlayStation 2 lets you watch movies, play games both solo and online with friends a state or continent away, the PSP lets you do the same, but on the road and without hooking up to a TV screen. You can't play PlayStation 2 games on the PSP, though – officially, only games developed specifically for the PSP in the Universal Media Disc (UMD) format can run on it. Unofficially? We'll get to that later.

Is the PSP the best portable gaming system available?

It's certainly one of the most popular, and developers – both legit companies and hackers – are working very hard to help PSP owners exploit the full potential of the machine. It's also by far the most versatile system, with its ability to play games off different media. And there is room for Sony to markedly improve the hardware by, for example, adding a micro hard drive or internal flash memory, which would raise it way above the competition.

There are a number of portable gaming machines on the market, ranging from Nintendo's Game Boy Advance to Nokia's N-Gage (primarily a phone), the closest thing to the PSP being the Nintendo DS and the recently released DS Lite. The DS boasts some features that the PSP currently lacks: a built-in microphone and microphone input, which allow users to chat with one another easily; a touch screen through which you can easily navigate menus, some games, and key in text; and not one but two screens. However, it doesn't have the PSP's more advanced capabilities, and aesthetically, it's rather clunky at over an inch thick when closed. Nintendo has addressed some of these issues with the newly released DS Lite, which comes in more colors, and has been shrunk in both size and price, costing somewhere around 70% of the PSP Core System. The PSP's single screen is still over 50% larger than the DS's two, however, and offers significantly higher resolution.

To find out more about how other brands compare, check out the product reviews at a site like amazon.com or amazon.co.uk. The rest of this book is going to focus only on the PSP.

What can it do besides play games and movies?

Think of the PSP as a funnel for nearly all forms of digital media – everything from video games to full-length films to MP3 music and podcasts can flow through the PSP. It's a surprisingly versatile device, thanks not only to the efforts of Sony, but also to the work done by third-party software providers and hackers. The first version of the PSP's operating system (or firmware; see p.109) allowed the machine to run software developed by anybody, not just Sony, and in the brief period before this hole was plugged, both hackers and developers realized the potential of the PSP – not as just a gaming system, but as a platform for all sorts of applications. There's now a fairly large cottage industry of developers and a community of hackers working on software for your PSP.

HACKING THE PSP

Not all "hackers" are bad. Of course there are plenty of virus-writers and other malevolent types looking for ways to permanently crash your computer, steal your personal data, and so forth, but there are good guys out there too. Often referred to as "white hat" hackers, they write programs that can trick your computer or other electronic device into doing things its designers neither expected nor planned for. Homebrew (see p.48) is one of these things. So when we talk about hacks, we don't mean viruses or anything else nasty – we're talking about shortcuts or innovative ways to get your PSP to do neat things.

More and more, the PSP is becoming able to do things a computer does; for instance, you can send email and surf the Internet using the inbuilt web browser. And if you don't really want to use it as a gaming device at all, there's even a program that turns your PSP into a Windows 95 computer (see p.140).

Some other things your PSP can do include:

• Play old Nintendo games via aNES emulator (see p.49).

- Create a photo slideshow (see p.87).
- Watch movies and TV shows over a WiFi connection (see p.158).
- Act like a Roland TB-303 bass sequencer (see p.134).
- Learn a foreign language with Talkman (see p.136).

So can the PSP replace my iPod?

Well, sort of, depending on what you want to get out of it. Apple's high-end iPods have hard disks as large as those of some computers. The PSP, with no onboard memory, just doesn't compete when it comes to storing your CD collection. The PSP is also bigger – a lot bigger.

But it's probably not so much a matter of replacing your iPod (or other digital music player), as it is of taking a look at what you want your digital devices to do for you, and buying the one that best fits your needs. Do you need video games? Buy the PSP, because the iPod games are awful. Do you need something small enough to fit neatly in the hip pocket of your skin-tight Joe's jeans? Buy an iPod nano.

Do I need a computer?

No. If all you want to do is watch UMD movies and play UMD games, keeping your game saves on a Memory Stick, the PSP is enough in itself.

But if you want to exploit the possibilities of the PSP – listening to MP3 songs and podcasts, playing emulators for older game systems, and more – you'll need a computer. Many of the PSP's advanced capabilities require that you download some kind of software for your computer and connect this with your PSP. See the next section for more information about what you need to make the most of your machine.

CONNECTING WITH A COMPUTER

You can use the PSP very easily with most computers provided you buy a compatible USB cable. One end of this cable is the standard USB connection that you can plug into any computer; the other is a mini connection that plugs into your PSP.

It's one crucial piece of equipment that doesn't come with the basic PSP packages (see p.12), but thankfully it's not a proprietary cable, so you can find it in the many and varied PSP accessories kits available, or you can just pop down to an electrical or computer store like Radio Shack or Currys and buy one for under ten dollars (or around £15). One of the writers of this book bought his; the other repurposed the cable that came with his minidisc recorder and it works just fine. If you do need to buy one, it's an excellent investment considering what it permits you to do with your PSP.

Armed with a cable, you can use the PSP with a computer running any operating system that recognizes external devices.

The hook-up

When you first plug in your PSP to your computer, nothing happens. In order to use the PSP's USB connection, you must first activate it. After you've plugged in

USB Connection

the PSP, move the cursor all the way to the left until you get to the **Settings** menu, then highlight **USB Connection** and select it with the X button.

Your Memory Stick light will flash, your PSP will display the text "USB Mode" and an image will mount on your computer's desktop.

What's happened is that the Mac has recognized your Memory Stick PRO Duo as a drive, and the PC has recognized it as an external device. As you would with a CD-R, a USB drive, or any other form of storage, you can just drag and drop files onto the Memory Stick. We recommend that you format your Memory Stick for your PSP before adding any files (see p.32 for instructions), but if you want or need to simply store anything immediately, go to it. It won't do any harm, but you probably won't be able to access the relevant file through your PSP.

As you might expect, the folders are for precisely what they say: photos (see p.85); games (see p.39); music (see p.75); and game saves (see p.192). (There's no folder labeled "movies" or "video," however – see the section starting on p.63 to find out how to store this kind of content.) Through your computer, you can manipulate the files on your Memory Stick, which allows you to do all sorts of things we get to later in the book. Note that the file folders are the same for Windows XP as they are for Mac OSX and any other operating system. In fact, the only issue for non-Windows users is that they won't be able to process audio files in

BASICS & BUYING

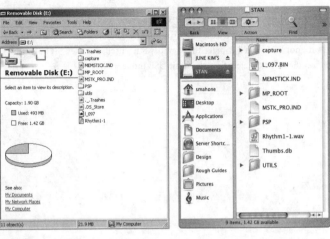

These are the file menus you see after formatting the Memory Stick. On the left, Windows XP. On the right, Mac OSX.

the ATRAC3 and ATRAC3plus formats, which are used by Sony's online music store.

But since third-party and homebrew software (see p.48) is written for the PSP's firmware, rather than your computer, you can download any of these files to your computer, whether it's running XP, OSX, or something else, and drop it into the appropriate file folder for use.

Before you disconnect the PSP from your Mac, you should first eject the drive by opening your hard disk menu and pressing the "eject" icon next to the Memory Stick icon. Alternatively, drag the icon to the Trash. Your PSP can now be safely unplugged from the computer. Similarly, with the PC, use the "Add/Remove Hardware" function in your "Settings" menu to safely disconnect the PSP from your computer.

TIP If you exit USB mode on the PSP before you "eject" the PSP from your computer, you run the risk of corrupting the data on your Memory Stick. It's not likely you'll damage the Memory Stick itself, nor the PSP, but to be on the safe side, eject first, then exit USB mode.

02

Buying a PSP

new or used? black or white?

You can find a PSP just about anywhere from Amazon to your neighborhood gaming store. With a couple of important exceptions (see below), there's not much to consider other than getting the best deal. The cost of a new PSP tends to be fairly standard, although doing some comparison shopping online and at major electronics retailers sometimes can yield modest savings or a bundle that's particularly well suited to your needs.

BUYING NEW

If you're buying new, there are three commonly available PSP systems at the time of writing, plus a host of other retailer-specific bundles.

Core System or Base Pack

The most basic pack comprises the PSP itself, the battery, and the power cord/adaptor, and retails for around $200/£145.

Value Pack

For around $250/£165, the Value Pack gets you the Core System/ Base Pack, plus headphones and remote control, a pouch, and a 32MB Memory Stick Duo. If you want a complete package that lets you get started right away, it's not a bad choice, though you might prefer to spend that extra $50 on a bigger Memory Stick from the outset.

Giga Pack

Less widely available than the previous two, this pack, usually costing about $300/£215, swaps the Value Pack's 32MB Memory Stick Duo for a 1GB Memory Stick Duo PRO and also throws in a handy USB cable. Getting all of this in one package, while convenient, may not be cost effective if Memory Sticks continue to plummet in price.

Other bundles

A slew of other bundles for the PSP exists through a wide variety of retailers. Some come with a film, a game or two, or even with external speakers to improve the PSP's sound. But we've found these to be rarely worth the premium – before handing over the cash, it's always worth checking that you can't buy the components cheaper separately.

BUYING USED

As with any purchase of used electronics, if you buy a secondhand PSP you bear some risk. Sony doesn't sell refurbished models of the PSP, although if your PSP dies and you get a replacement, you might receive a refurbished device. New PSPs come with a one-year limited warranty that will get you repair or replacement if your PSP suffers from mechanical defects. With used machines, though, you have no guarantee, unless you have the original bill of sale and it's less than a year old. Otherwise, if you encounter any problems, you're on your own.

However, you can find some good deals in the used marketplace, and sometimes even get certain kinds of guarantees – largely against fradulent sales. For example, if you buy a PSP on eBay that doesn't work, you may be able to get your money refunded. Amazon and eBay are the two behemoths of online used goods, but they're not the only places to find used PSPs – try a video game shop, or looking through classifieds (be they in newspapers or online).

BASICS & BUYING

DOES IT COME IN OTHER COLORS?

Until recently the only PSP sold in the English-speaking parts of the world was the standard black one that you see on the cover of this book. However, Sony released a "ceramic white" PSP in the Japanese market that in 2006 was subsequently released in the UK, retailing for around £180 and sometimes bundled with a game or two. You can't buy one in the US through normal channels, although they're easily found online, either used – at prices that vary wildly – or new, from Far East suppliers.

Note that UMD games are region-free, which means that North Americans who manage to get hold of a ceramic white PSP will be able to buy local games for it. Movies are a different story – you would need to import Region 2 UMDs – unless, of course, you only watch films you've converted to MP4 files (see p.66).

WHICH FIRMWARE VERSION?

If you're shopping for PSPs online you'll notice the emphasis placed on firmware, which is basically the operating system of the PSP. We discuss firmware later in the book, but the version of firmware your PSP runs determines to a large extent what it can do – see pp.112–113 for a chart.

USING THE
PSP

△
□
○
✕

03

The hardware

what's in the box

Getting to know the basics of your PSP isn't very difficult, but a more detailed understanding of how your PSP works, what it includes, what cables you need, and what UMDs and Memory Sticks are all about, is crucial for everything from basic gaming through advanced use. Here we define the terms used to discuss various aspects of the PSP – turn back to this section if you're not sure what's meant by "the X button," for example. Let's start with what you get when you open the box.

The PSP unit

Chapter 3

1 Directional buttons: Up, Down, Right, Left Sometimes called the D-pad, these buttons are used to move video game characters around the screen and to navigate menus.

2 Shoulder buttons: Left, Right Most often used in gaming and to scroll through photo slideshows.

3 Memory Stick Duo indicator Lights up when the Memory Stick is in use.

TIP When the Memory Stick Duo indicator is lit, DO NOT remove the Memory Stick. Removing it while the indicator is lit may damage both the Memory Stick and your PSP, and is certain to corrupt your data.

4 WLAN indicator Lights up when the PSP is using its wireless access feature.

5 Analog stick A smoother, more responsive alternative to the D-pad, used in games, and also functions like a mouse or trackpad in the PSP's web browser.

6 Home button Pressing this gives you the option to return to the PSP's main (Home) menu.

7 Volume buttons Turns the volume down and up.

⑧ Display button Adjusts the brightness level of the LCD screen through four consecutive levels, the brightest of which is only available when the PSP is plugged into the AC adaptor.

⑨ Sound button Adjusts the tone of the sound. The tone can only be adjusted when using headphones to listen to music or movies, but not when playing games.

⑩ Select button Varies depending on the game.

⑪ Start button Used to start games, and to pause games and films.

⑫ Hold indicator Turns a yellow color when the Power Switch is slid into the "hold" position.

⑬ Power indicator Shows green when the PSP is on and flashes green when the battery charge is low. Shows orange when the PSP's battery is charging until fully charged.

⑭ Square, Triangle, Circle, and X buttons Perform various functions depending on the operation of the PSP. Generally, X selects or activates an option or moves you to a submenu, circle cancels an operation or takes you back to the previous menu, and pressing triangle will display an options pallette. A notable exception occurs in game emulators, where circle will load the game.

Chapter 3

① IR port Used for IR communication;
currently underutilized by the PSP.

② USB socket

③ Open latch Slide to the right to open the UMD door.

④ Memory Stick Duo slot

⑤ Headphone jack and PSP headset/remote socket Plug your headphones and PSP
headset or remote in here.

⑥ DC-in and charging terminals Plug in your AC adaptor here. The charging terminals are
used when the PSP is connected to other devices or base stations that will also charge
the battery (see p.152).

7 Power switch Used to turn your PSP on and off, and to put it to sleep. To turn the PSP on, just slide the switch up. To turn it off, slide the switch up and hold it in place for about three seconds. To put it to sleep, slide it up for just a moment.

8 WLAN switch Used to turn wireless networking on and off.

> **TIP** If your PSP freezes, slide the power switch up and hold it in place for ten seconds or so. The PSP will shut down, and you can restart it as normal.

21

USING THE PSP

Batteries and power supplies

The battery pack that powers the PSP claims to give around 6 hours of use, although this time varies according to what you're doing with it. Using the WiFi connection while playing a UMD game will drain the battery at a quicker rate, but if you're listening to MP3s with headphones on and the screen turned off, the charge will last a while longer. For tips on extending battery life, see p.166.

The AC adaptor and the AC power cord are used to charge the PSP battery. As with the batteries themselves, there are also third-party products available, such as power packs that can charge your PSP on the go. For more details, turn to p.153.

Headphones and remote control

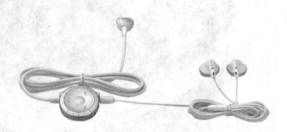

At the time of writing, the Sony PSP remote (as included in the Value Pack and Giga Pack) is the only one that works with the PSP, controlling video and audio content you've stored on the Memory Stick, as well as UMD films. You can, however, substitute your own headphones for the PSP's basic set; either can be plugged directly into the remote or the device.

Sony also makes the PSP headset, designed to support the game SOCOM: Fire Team Bravo, in which you can talk to other players. This inbuilt support for voice communication signals some potential for the PSP's future use as a telephony device . . .

USING THE PSP

23

THE MEMORY STICK

Some packs will include a Memory Stick, which you'll need for game saves and playing your own media. See the Memory Stick chapter beginning on p.29 for an in-depth look at its functions.

04

The Universal Media Disc

movies, games, music

Like a CD, DVD, or minidisc, the Universal Media Disc (hereafter referred to as UMD), is an optical disc storing digital data, which is read by a laser and translated by the PSP into content – most likely a movie or video game. The UMD can hold up to 1.8 gigabytes of data, more than enough for a feature-length film at the video resolution that the PSP offers.

Using UMDs

Like most things that Sony develops, the UMD is a proprietary format. Nevertheless, UMDs have a decent storage capacity, so until Sony figures out a way to distribute copy-protected software and content you can use off of flash memory, it looks like they're here to stay. Hence, blank UMDs aren't available except to movie distributors and game manufacturers. This makes it harder to copy UMD films or games, but only slightly. See pp.65 and 46 for information on backing up your UMD movies and games.

UMDs are small, the disc itself measuring only around 2.36 inches or 60mm in diameter, but fixed into a slightly larger transparent and white plastic casing, through which you can see the label with information on the game or movie.

WHO'S MAKING GAMES?

Since the PSP's debut, nearly every major game developer has thrown its hat into the ring, producing games that in many cases signify a step up from traditional handheld game fodder. Versions of hugely popular titles have been ported to the PSP – Mortal Kombat, Grand Theft Auto, Madden football, Pro Evolution soccer, and more. The PSP, at least for now, is a growth area for third-party developers, and will probably remain so, considering that Sony's game development arms haven't stepped up with many killer games themselves. Over three-fourths of software revenue generated by the PSP has gone to third-party software firms. In contrast, over half the software revenue generated by the Nintendo DS has gone directly to Nintendo, a company with a much longer history of game development.

Some of the major companies involved in PSP development include:

Activision	Koei	Rockstar
Atari	Konami	Sega
Bandai	LucasArts	THQ
Capcom	Midway	Ubisoft
Electronic Arts	Namco	

Take care when removing the UMD from its shrunken DVD-style case. There's no protective slide over the data surface of the disk, leaving it exposed to the elements, or more likely, your fingernails if you accidentally grab it the wrong way. The best way to remove the UMD is to press down on the bottom right corner – on the icon resembling a PlayStation controller or a film frame – until it pops out of its restraints. It can be clicked back into the box in the same way.

ADULT CONTENT

Although Sony has publicly announced that it finds it "utterly undesirable," a variety of pornographic films are readily available on UMD. Information may want to be free, but pornography wants to be on all media it possibly can, and to charge you for such masterpieces as Japan's "Erotic Terrorist Beautiful Body" or the UK's "Desperately Sexy Housewives."

UMD GAMES

The big market for the PSP, of course, is the gaming community. Just about every recent popular game is available for the PSP, with some titles developed specifically for the system. The PSP has been selling at about the same rate as the Nintendo DS, currently the only other machine in the PSP's class. At press time, over 120 games were available for the PSP, and at least a handful of new games are released each month.

While the number and quality of future releases depend somewhat on demand, with a base of over 15 million users to satisfy, corporate game development for the PSP is expected to flourish, at least for a few years.

UMD REGIONS

Just like DVDs, UMDs have region encoding. Look on your PSP box for a square with rounded corners, inside which is a portion of a globe-like object and a number.

Both UMD games and movies are encoded, but thus far Sony has only enabled the encoding on movies – games produced for any region will work on any PSP, at least for now. That is to say, if you want to order a game from Japan that's not available in the US, for example, you will be able to play it, although you might want to check that it can run in English. However, region encoding can interfere with multiplayer gaming. A gamer running a Japanese version of a game won't necessarily be able to play against a gamer running a US version of the same game. It's unclear whether this affects the titles with game sharing, but at this point few games have this feature anyway.

Sony's relevant UMD encoding is as follows:

Region 0/All Open format

Region 1 US and Canada

Region 2 Japan, European Union, Middle East (including Egypt), South Africa

Region 3 Southeast Asia

Region 4 Australia, New Zealand, Pacific Islands, Mexico, Central and South America, Caribbean nations

Region 5 Russia, Eastern Europe (including former Soviet Republics), the Indian subcontinent, Africa (excluding Egypt and South Africa), North Korea, and Mongolia

Region 6 China

For multiplayer games and for movies, it's safest to play only games and UMDs that are encoded for your region, or, more appropriately, encoded for the same region as your PSP. So if you imported a Japanese PSP, it's safest to stick to Region 2 games and films.

UMD FILMS

Films on the PSP are downright impressive. UMDs truly provide DVD-quality video, and the screen is exceptionally crisp for a portable device. On the other hand, as played through the PSP's external speakers, UMD films sound universally dreadful, although using headphones can raise the bar from passable (with the PSP headphones) to pretty good. Hundreds of movies have been released on UMD, almost all of them from major studios, and the UMD catalog is still expanding, if more cautiously than before.

That's because UMD films are widely considered to be a commercial failure. Despite the hundreds of films available, and their high quality, consumers aren't biting. Maybe they're annoyed that in order to watch films they already own on the PSP, they have to pony up as much as or even more than the original DVDs. So instead, they copy their DVD onto their computer, convert it into MP4 format, and drop it on a high-capacity Memory Stick (see p.68).

But if you do want to spend that money, you can find UMD films at most major electronics and music/DVD retailers, as well as at many video game stores. You can find a list of currently available UMD movies at the following sites.

PlayStation www.us.playstation.com/psp/umdmovies.aspx?all
Official PSP www.yourpsp.co.uk/psp/psp.html
The Digital Bits www.thedigitalbits.com/articles/umdguide

05

The Memory Stick
saving & storing

Flash memory is the wave of the future. The expensive wave of the future. A high-capacity – and still fairly high-cost – way of storing data and moving it between devices, it's used in pretty much all portable electronic equipment, from digital cameras to cell phones to the PSP. Memory is one of the biggest issues for the PSP. Rumors have flown for some time about Sony introducing an internal microdrive or internal flash memory, but whether they will respond to consumer demand remains to be seen. Until they do, the Memory Stick is the primary way to save your games and store movies, music, and photos.

HOW IT WORKS

The PSP uses a form of flash memory called the Memory Stick PRO Duo, currently manufactured only by Sony and SanDisk. It's smaller and faster than the original, widely used Memory Stick

Chapter 5

products, indeed fast enough to directly record DVD-quality video. Which also means it's possible to transfer large files, such as movies, to the Memory Stick PRO Duo at reasonable speeds. As with USB drives, which are also flash memory, you can save any data you want on the Memory Stick – MP3 files and movies, but also ROMs for game emulators and documents as well.

Even if you only intend to use your PSP for games, you still need a Memory Stick PRO Duo (or an adaptor that lets you use other memory – see p.155), because unlike, say, a Game Boy cartridge, the UMD is fixed media – you can't record or erase any data such as saved games on it.

> Although the Memory Stick and the Memory Stick PRO Duo are separate products, for simplicity's sake, we use the term "Memory Stick" throughout the rest of this book. Please don't make the mistake of buying a regular Memory Stick because of this! Only Memory Stick PRO Duo will work with the PSP.

A number of products, generally Sony products, store information right on the Memory Stick. VAIO computers, for example, come with a slot for the Memory Stick. And if you use a Sony camera with a Memory Stick formatted for the PSP, your pictures will save in a folder called "Digital Camera Images" and be immediately available on the PSP should you swap the Stick back into the device. The newest Micro Sticks – as used in Sony mobile phones – don't have an adaptor for the PSP yet, so in that case, you're out of luck.

CHOOSING A MEMORY STICK

You should buy either as little memory as you can get away with or as much as you can afford – take your choice. Depending on which system you've purchased (see p.11 for the basic options), you may already have either a 32MB or 1GB Memory Stick PRO Duo. If you've gone for the Core System (in the US) or the Basic Pack (in the UK), you need to take a Memory Stick PRO Duo home, too.

If you're only interested in watching UMD movies and playing UMD games, then our advice is to spend as little money as you can. At time of writing, it was easy to find 256MB Sticks for under $30/£18 both online and in stores, and this price is sure to drop as bigger capacity sticks continue to arrive on the market. Game saves take up hardly any space, and a 256MB Stick will still leave you with enough room for about three hours of music.

If you want to do more with your PSP – like watching copies of movies that you've made from your own DVDs, for example – you'll want the biggest Memory Stick PRO Duo you can afford. The larger Sticks are more costly, but you may find it's worth it to have a large music collection on your PSP, or to take multiple movies on a trip in the smallest package possible.

The folks over at CNET's Gamespot (**www.gamespot.com**) have done some comparative speed tests between Sony and SanDisk Memory Sticks, and they found that the SanDisk products were markedly faster – almost three times faster, in fact. Considering that SanDisk Memory Sticks are also usually at least 10% cheaper, we're happy to go with their recommendation.

> **TIP** While all forms of flash memory are very stable, they also tend to be a bit fragile. Don't touch the connectors (the metal strips at one end of your Memory Stick), as dirt and oil from your skin can interfere with data transfer. Don't bend your Memory Stick. Also, the PSP's Memory Stick is really small. Keep it away from children who like to put things in their mouths. It's bad for them, and you'll probably lose all of your data.

FORMATTING THE MEMORY STICK

The PSP manual has clear instructions about inserting and removing your Memory Stick – we'll assume you understand them. Once you've successfully inserted your Memory Stick, you'll see that a Memory Stick-shaped icon appears under each of the relevant menu items – Game, Video, Music, Photo.

When you get a new Memory Stick, we advise formatting it for your PSP right away. It'll set up your Memory Stick in a standard way that becomes crucial if you want to utilize some of the advanced capabilities we explore later on. You can alter its settings later (or swap it out for a different Memory Stick) as you learn more about what you need your PSP to do.

First, put your Memory Stick into your PSP and power up. Navigate from the **Home** menu to **System Settings** and select it with the X button. Scroll down to **Format Memory Stick** and select it. Select **Yes** when you're asked "Do you want to format the Memory Stick?" The PSP will then ask, "All data on the Memory Stick will be deleted. Are you sure you want to continue?" The PSP is not kidding – if you have things on your Memory Stick from another device, or game saves from friends, or anything you don't want to lose, we strongly recommend backing up your Memory Stick. Otherwise, say goodbye to your data. So if you're sure, move the cursor over "Yes" again, and press X. The PSP will tell you not to remove your Memory Stick or turn off the power. Obey your PSP. When finished, the PSP will tell you "Format Completed." Pressing the circle button will take you back to the main menu.

The PSP will have created folders called **GAME**, **MUSIC**, **PHOTO**, **COMMON**, and **MP_ROOT**. The first three are for exactly what they say they're for. **COMMON** is the catchall folder for the PSP – if it doesn't know where to put something, such as a Word document you've downloaded, it goes into the **COMMON** folder. **MP_ROOT** has a few different uses, but by far the most frequent is as the folder for your digital videos – see p.71 for details.

33

SAVING YOUR STICK

Backing up your Memory Stick before trying new or advanced processes with your PSP is always a good idea. To do this manually, create a folder on your computer called "Mem Stick Backup" or the like. Then "Select All" the contents of your Memory Stick and paste them into that folder. If your Memory Stick somehow gets corrupted, you can delete all of its contents, "Select All" the files from your "Mem Stick Backup" folder, and paste them back onto the Memory Stick. It should be as good as new!

06

Additional content
keeping it legal

Digital rights management is an enormous issue for media companies today. Ever since the first incarnation of Napster broke online distribution of music wide open, companies that create digital media – record labels, movie studios, software developers, and others – have been struggling to secure their products against illegal copying and distribution. For example, Sony secures music purchased from their Connect store with an encryption technology called MagicGate, which only computers and specified devices like your PSP can decrypt. Nevertheless, there exists a thriving community of file-sharers who illegally distribute and download music, movies, software, and other copyrighted digital products. File-sharing itself is not against the law, but distributing and downloading copyrighted content without permission is.

Throughout this book, we describe processes, computer programs, and websites that help you use your PSP to consume and use media that you already own in another format. Certainly, some of what we discuss could be put to illegal use. If you choose to copy your UMD games or movies, or to change your DVDs into video files for the PSP, or to convert your copy-protected iTunes tracks into unprotected MP3s, please only do so for back-up purposes or for your personal use. Sharing (or worse, selling) backup UMDs, digital movies, or MP3s is almost certainly illegal. Make sure you understand the relevant laws of your country and/or territory, or you may be held liable for substantial financial damages should you be caught.

Sony's shields: MagicGate & DNAS

Sony uses an encryption system called MagicGate to handle its digital rights management issues. If you buy music from Sony's online music store, Connect, you receive files that are encrypted with MagicGate. In order to play these files, you need to have a device that authenticates the songs – like the PSP, a PS2, your Windows computer, or one of Sony's digital Walkmans. MagicGate helps Sony prevent the illegal distribution of these downloads.

Since the Memory Stick and the PSP both use MagicGate, you can play songs from the Sony Connect store on your PSP. At press time, games and films weren't being sold with this kind of encoding, but Sony's PSOne download service is certain to feature protection measures – probably using MagicGate.

DNAS (Dynamic Network Authentication System) is Sony's proprietary system created to regulate online gameplay originally for the for the PS2 and now used for the PSP. DNAS has had some good effects – for example, it helps keep people who have hacked cheats into their games out of the online gaming community. A downside of DNAS for game pirates is that it authenticates the game and checks for copy protection before letting you online.

Which means that it's much harder to play illegally copied games online, although not impossible. Searching online for "DNAS patch" will yield a trove of information on the ways to do this for the PS2. We have yet to hear about a patch for the PSP, but certainly one is in the works.

The risks and rewards of PSP hacks

You can do numerous things with your PSP that Sony would prefer you didn't. Copying your own DVDs into viewable files instead of buying the UMD of the same film, for example. Doing this won't cause you any problems with regard to getting your PSP repaired should something go wrong, but a slew of other things this book discusses will instantly render your PSP warranty null and void.

As it turns out, voiding your warranty is really pretty easy. Downgrading your firmware (see p.115)? Running homebrew software (see p.124)? Replacing your PSP's faceplate with a custom one (see p.148)? Voided warranty! All of these things can be done without causing your PSP any harm, and later in this book we'll tell you how. But you should know upfront that if you do pretty much anything other than what's described in Sony's manual (with the exception of playing video files, which is permitted but poorly explained), you stand a good chance of voiding your warranty.

But the rewards may be worth it to you. If you get emulators (programs that allow you to play video games from legacy systems like the Sega Genesis) up and running, you can play your old favorites. Voided warranty? Yup. Illegal? Maybe – see p.50 for a discussion of legal issues about emulators. Fun? For sure. Other homebrew programs allow you to use your PSP as everything from a drum machine to a universal remote. Sony naturally feels very strongly that you shouldn't run these "unauthorized programs" on hardware of their design, but that's not to say they won't enhance your PSP experience – and if Sony's not going to create them, then others certainly will.

GAMES

△
□
○
✕

07

UMD games

shake it, don't break it

Great games can make or break a videogame system. The Sega Dreamcast and the Atari Jaguar both went the way of the dodo – as good as these systems were, without the suppport of the big-name games publishers, they soon became evolutionary rejects. The PlayStation's vast library of proven games encourages the best developers to invest their time and resources into creating games that could potentially sell hundreds of thousands of copies on the PSP. Genre-defining series like Grand Theft Auto and SOCOM have been brought to the PSP, while PC games and 8-bit classics have been resurrected for a new life in UMD form. Read on for a rundown of the best UMD games currently available, and some tips on multiplayer gaming and backing up your UMDs.

Chapter 7

WHAT'S OUT THERE?

Naturally, the games with the highest audiovisual quality, greatest complexity, and finest game play are the UMD games designed specifically for the PSP. The following list is a collection of the games that make us play until our thumbs bleed. If you want to try out or simply go ahead and buy any of these games, check the Resources section for a list of options (see p.189).

Sports	Strategy	Shooter	Racing	Role Playing	Action/Adventure

Burnout Legends
Electronic Arts

Super fast cars and explosion on impact make for a thrilling ride. There are eight different play modes, numerous tracks, and you can even race against UMD-less friends in a gamesharing demo version.

Capcom Puzzle World
Capcom Ad Hoc

Challenge a friend to a block-breaking or gem-smashing competition in one of Capcom's classics: Super Puzzle Fighter II, Block Block, or the Buster Brothers Collection. While your friend is in the lavatory, upload your high scores to his machine using the built-in Ad Hoc feature.

Daxter
Sony Computer Entertainment Ad Hoc

Featuring smooth controls and gorgeous graphics, the ottsel of Jak & Daxter fame goes solo, armed with an electrified flyswatter and a bug spray.

GTA: Liberty City Stories
Rockstar Games

This version of Grand Theft Auto is just as immersive and compelling as the other

editions of the game. Driving the familiar roads of Liberty City feels like a homecoming, especially while the Triads are filling your Rumpo full of lead.

Lemmings
Sony Computer Entertainment

If you haven't tried to stop a mass suicide before, now's your chance. Lemmings is an Amiga classic that's been made available on over 20 systems through the years, including mobile phones and PDAs along with PCs and the Gamegear. The PSP version adds a level editor where you can create new boards to challenge yourself and your friends.

Lumines
Ubisoft

Breaking blocks has changed quite a bit since Breakout!, with Tetris the first in the newwave of shape-strategy games to introduce moving pieces. Lumines may not be a true next-gen strategy game, but its challenging screens, responsive music, and multiplayer capabilities make it an addictive source of entertainment.

Me and My Katamari
Namco

Like a snowball rolling down the side of a mountain, your katamari can absorb matter from one area and then distribute it somewhere else. Watch out for living creatures though – if you haven't reached sufficient mass, an ape could kick you off the screen.

MLB '06: The Show
Sony Computer Entertainment

Play in career mode as a single player making your way through the big leagues team by team, or back an entire roster and shoot for the pennant. You can also recruit from dozens of classic players, letting you field a team where A-Rod bats third, and the Babe cleans up.

41

Chapter 7

Mega Man Powered Up
Capcom

Relive the very first Nintendo version, with a PSP-powered graphics boost and a construction mode that lets you build levels for uploading to the Powered Up community.

Monster Hunter Freedom
Capcom

Slash and shoot your way through a dizzying array of highly stylized monsters while your experience builds and your skills increase. Don't forget to relax with a bit of fishing and gardening.

Ridge Racer
Namco

This arcade standard introduced us to the Nitro boost and Reiko Nagase, perhaps the most beautifully articulated race car driver known to man. The PSP version contains more racetracks than any other version in the series, though you'll have to unlock them as you improve your standing in World Tour Mode.

SOCOM: U.S. Navy SEALs Fireteam Bravo 2
Sony Computer Entertainment

Hunt and kill your friends and neighbors, and get away with it. SOCOM continues its reign as the best shooter for the PlayStation consoles, with WiFi support for a full sixteen players battling at once, and a special headset (see p.23) that lets you bark orders at unruly teammates.

Superman Returns: The Videogame
Electronic Arts

Keep Metropolis safe while impressing Lois Lane with your form-fitting suit and majestically flowing cape. Challenges can be approached and solved in numerous different ways, as should be the case for someone who can fly, lift 100 tons, and shoot heat beams from his eyes.

Super Monkey Ball Adventure
Sega

A strategy game gone safari. Use a variety of differently abled balls to navigate the troop through scrolling levels, with – as a flashback to previous versions – fifty odd puzzles to solve along the way.

Syphon Filter: Dark Mirror
Sony Computer Entertainment

Ad Hoc   Infrastructure

A quality mission-based shooter in story mode, the real fun happens in multiplayer mode, where even your best friend becomes a target for your bloodlust. Online victory gains you badges, weapons, and bragging rights.

43

Tales of Eternia
Ubisoft

Choose your character and set off on a heroic quest for maximum hit points in the PSP's best RPG so far. You can also stop the game mid-mission and save, a very handy feature that's unique to the PSP version.

Tiger Woods PGA Tour
Electronic Arts

Ad Hoc

Play some of the world's finest courses as Tiger Woods, or as your own creation complete with customized clothes and hair style. As you win tournaments you'll earn money to buy better clubs and swankier clothes – show off your new duds and 300 yard drive the next time your Ad Hoc foursome hits the links.

GAMES

Tony Hawk's Underground 2 Remix
Activision

The birdman lands on the PSP. Master the 900 and the benihanna while you thrash through the story mode courses. Multiplayer games are standard fare, but you do get to tag a few walls in the graffiti game.

Virtua Tennis: World Tour
Sega Ad Hoc

Simple to learn, difficult to master. Updating the Dreamcast version with the likes of Sharipova, this addictive PSP sports sim will push you toward overdose.

Winning Eleven 9/ProEvolution Soccer 5
Konami Ad Hoc

This PS2 standout brings to the PSP realistic gameplay based on lifelike body movements, ball dynamics, and a frustrating inability to put away the winner. Unfortunately, the Master League mode was too big to fit, so you're stuck with regular league play and cup matches only.

Wipeout Pure
Sony Computer Entertainment

Before GTA, this was the game that made us drive too fast, weave through traffic, and hover a few feet off the ground. Pure fun, and more (see p.100).

X-Men Legends II: Rise of Apocalypse
Activision

Play with a group of four mutants chosen from the ranks of the X-Men and Brotherhood of Evil Mutants on your mission to defeat the power-mad En Sabah Nur. You can make a multiplayer affair of it with friends in the same room, or strangers across the Internet.

GAMES

44

MULTIPLAYER GAMING

Playing head-to-head has been one of the coolest features of portable gaming ever since we whipped our friends at Tetris using a wired connection between Game Boys. The PSP offers two ways to play with other PSP owners, using a wireless connection referred to as either WiFi or WLAN (Wireless Local Area Network).

Ad Hoc gameplay

For certain games your PSP can create an Ad Hoc network, a local network that allows PSPs to talk to each other – and thus enables head-to-head gameplay – without logging on to the Internet. Check your UMD game box to see if it supports Ad Hoc multiplayer gaming. If it does, all you need to do is start up your game and turn on your WLAN switch. The game will give you a **Multiplayer** option – select it, and you can either join an existing game or host one yourself. Whomever you're playing with will need to have the same game running on their PSP as well. You can network up to sixteen PSPs this way, but the number of people who can play any given game is defined by the game itself.

Infrastructure Mode

Multiplayer gaming in Infrastructure Mode means using an Internet connection to play against people anywhere in the world. Getting your PSP online can be as easy as turning on the WLAN switch – or a lot more tricky. See the Networking section beginning on p.91 for more details.

Unlike Microsoft with its Xbox Live, Sony doesn't have a centralized network for you to play across; rather, it's totally dependent on the game and its manufacturer as to whether you can play it online and what kind of support exists. If your game does support Infrastructure Mode – and a number do, particularly sports titles, but also the popular SOCOM and Syphon Filter games – you'll need to turn on your WLAN switch and select **Infrastructure** from the game's multiplayer options menu. What happens next is, again, totally dependent on the game. Most require that you create some kind of online identity. The game company's network will then run a DNAS check on your game to make sure that you haven't hacked it with cheats that give you an unfair advantage, and that you're not trying to use an illegal copy of a UMD game.

BACKING UP YOUR UMDS

The UMD may be a well-protected proprietary format, but it's still possible to back up UMD games and films to your computer. A handful of programs exist that allow you to copy UMDs and to load and run their content on your PSP from the Memory Stick, a process that's often called "dumping," since it copies the exact contents of the UMD onto your computer or Memory Stick without doing anything else to the files.

In order to do any of this, you must be running version 1.50 of the PSP firmware – no UMD backup program will work with PSPs running other versions. Your 1.50 PSP is probably no longer under warranty, but if it is, you will definitely void that warranty by running one of these programs; what's more, depending on where you live, circumventing copy protection – which this process does – may be illegal. Although these programs utilize fairly advanced techniques, they do come with excellent instructions in their readme.txt files, which you'll receive if you decide to go ahead and download them. All are available at **www.psp-hacks.com**.

Dumping and loading programs

One of the best programs for copying UMDs is **Fast Loader**, which dumps copies of UMDs directly onto your Memory Stick.

From there, you'll probably want to transfer these fairly large files to your computer for storage, moving them back onto your Memory Stick only when you need them.

When it comes to playing your backups, two programs exist that help you do this fairly smoothly – **UMD Emulator** and **DAX ZISO Loader**, both of which let you load the files as though they were actual UMDs; you usually need to have a UMD inserted in the PSP in order to run these programs.

Both programs incorporate **Run UMD** (see p.59), which should enable you to play backups of some newer UMD games on a PSP running 1.50.

GAMES

47

08

Homebrew games & emulators

retro gaming

PSP gaming isn't entirely about new-generation UMD games boasting state-of-the-art motion capture, real-life physics engines, and the like. Thanks to the flaw that allowed the first versions of the PSP's firmware to easily run unsigned code, a number of homebrew games have been written for the PSP, as well as conversions of games originally designed for the PC. Emulator programs are available, too, allowing you to play games released for older systems – like the original Legend of Zelda or Final Fantasy (both designed for the NES) – on your PSP. And if you have a more recent version of the firmware or if you have a newer PSP you can still join in the fun – see p.56 for info on eLoader, a program that helps run homebrew programs.

HOMEBREW GAMES

"Homebrew" is the term used to cover independently produced software that's not endorsed by Sony. Homebrew in general and how to run it on your PSP are discussed extensively in the relevant chapter (see p.124); here, we deal just with games.

Homebrew games take two forms: original works, of which there are rather few, and games converted or "ported" from other platforms, usually the PC. Amongst original homebrew offerings are games such as Casino Addict (a collection of casino-type games), 2D Paintball, and Skater Maze (a 2D game in which you must avoid thugs and collect enough coins to get a bus home). All of these are pretty simple, especially when compared to sophisticated "ports" like Quake, Doom, Duke Nukem, and even "Who Wants to Be a Millionaire?". Being able to take a multiplayer Quake game on the road was not something we'd expected to be able to do with the PSP, but it's a pretty great feature.

Most homebrew games, whether originals or ports, run best on version 1.50 of the PSP's firmware. If your PSP has version 2.00 through 2.60, your best bet is a program called eLoader (see p.56). For more on homebrew games and where to find them, see p.126.

EMULATORS

Emulators are applications that allow you to play games from old, long abandoned systems, such as the original Nintendo Entertainment System and Sega Genesis, on your PSP. Around since at least the late 1990s, they've been generally written for PCs, but now with the PSP you can take emulators with you on a device explicitly designed for gaming. This is one of the PSP's coolest features, and while its legality is up for debate (see overleaf), a tremendous amount of effort has gone into developing programs and workarounds that allow you to load emulators and play these legacy games on the PSP.

There are any number of emulators available to download, one of the best being "Yet Another Homebrew Pack," or **YAHP**, which comes in different editions for each version of firmware. The packs for versions 2.00 and above include eLoader, a program you need to run homebrew anyway, thereby saving you from having to download it separately.

Emulator programs are fundamentally the same, regardless of which version of firmware you're running, although not all emulators will work on all firmware. It's vital, then, to check that whichever emulator you're planning to use is proven to work with your version of firmware – you can find this out from the download site or in the "readme.txt" file included with the emulator itself.

> **TIP** If you have game saves or other data you don't want to lose, make sure you back up your Memory Stick by copying its contents onto your computer before loading up on homebrew. Homebrew – in fact, any software, really – can have glitches, and you don't want to risk losing valuable game progress just because you're impatient to start playing Super Mario Brothers.

Is this legal?

Digital rights management is a major issue for the creators and publishers of music, movies, and software, and it's rapidly becoming one for legacy video games, too. The problem in this case isn't with the emulator programs themselves, but with the actual games they enable you to play. These come in the form of computer files known as ROMs (due to the fact that they're copied from the original game cartridge's Read-Only Memory chip). By US law, you're allowed to own ROMs for which you possess the original game, and in the UK you're allowed to repurpose computer programs in order to make them work on another system; this so-called interoperability is precisely what ROM use permits. But there isn't readily available technology to help you convert your old NES games, say, to ROMs, so most people turn to the Internet for backups of the games they own – as well as for ROMs they don't (which is unequivocally illegal).

Where things get complicated is that, even if owning the ROM backup is legal in itself, you're not likely to be able to restore your copy of Zelda if something goes wrong with it – unless you have the equipment to manufacture a new NES cartridge, that is. The only way you can play it is through an emulator. But whether you're entitled to do this remains legally murky.

Nintendo claims that downloading and/or possessing ROMs, as well as the devices that allow you to copy the software onto computers, are illegal, and requests that anything that allows you to copy cartridges or to download or play ROMs be reported to them. How you would then make or acquire an archival copy of a video game you own – something that even they admit is your legal right – isn't clear.

That said, Nintendo's concern about their intellectual property being duplicated and spread around the Internet is well-founded. A quick search of any torrent site will bring up an astonishing number of ROMs. And in most cases, downloading them puts you in – at the very least – a legally tenuous position.

How to run an emulator

While emulators aren't themselves firmware specific, the way in which you get these programs to run on your PSP is. There are three different methods, depending on which version of firmware your PSP has.

Version 1.50

Running emulators with version 1.50 of the firmware, along with any other homebrew for that matter, is a breeze. Provided a program is written correctly, you can easily run it on your PSP.

> **TIP** For technical reasons that go beyond the remit of this book, homebrew programs for version 1.50 come as two folders, one of which ends in "…%". You can ignore these second folders, but don't delete them – if you do, your program won't run.

Once you've downloaded the emulator you'd like to play, hook your PSP up to your computer and put it in USB mode. Then simply drag or paste your emulator folders into the Memory Stick's **Game** folder.

Now that you have your emulator folders in the right place, you need to add some game ROMs in order to actually play any games. Simply drag or paste the ROM into the emulator folder on the Memory Stick. When you're done, eject the PSP from your computer, cancel USB mode, and disconnect the PSP.

All you have to do now is navigate to the **Game ▸ Memory Stick** menu, and you'll see listed any emulators you've put on your Memory Stick. Select an emulator and you'll get a very basic file menu showing you the games you have available as ROM files. The emulator often tells you which buttons on your PSP correspond to which buttons on the original gaming system. To start a game, select the ROM, press whichever button the emulator indicates will launch the ROM (usually circle), and your game will start up.

- GAME
  - capture
  - capture%
  - dgen_psp_120
  - IRSHELL
  - IRSHELL%
  - NesterJ_v1_11
  - PSPCHESS
  - PSPRadio
  - PSPRadio%
  - REMOTE
  - RHYTHM
  - SNES9X
  - Spider

To return to the regular PSP menu, simply press the Home button. As with UMD games, the PSP will ask you if you want to quit your game. Select yes, and you're back to the menu.

> **TIP** Once you've launched an emulator, loading a ROM works the same regardless of which firmware you have.

Version 2.00

Emulators don't work as easily on version 2.00 of the firmware. If you put emulators on your Memory Stick as detailed above, they'll certainly appear when you navigate to Game ▸ Memory Stick; however, when you try to run them, you'll receive the message "This game cannot be started. The data is corrupted."

Don't panic – your data isn't really corrupted. But in order to run the emulator you've downloaded – or any other homebrew, for that matter – you need a program called eLoader. See p.56 for instructions on getting eLoader up and running.

Once you've done that, connect your PSP to your computer in USB mode, copy the emulator folder to the Game folder on your Memory Stick, and drag or paste any game ROMs into the emulator folder. Eject your PSP from the computer, disconnect it, and navigate to the PSP's **Photo** menu. If you've installed eLoader correctly, there should be a folder there called "eLoader 096" (or 095, or 097, etc., depending on the version of eLoader you're using). Select the folder, press the X button, and wait a few seconds. Your screen will flash to black, and then you'll get a menu screen with some text on the left that has the names of various emulators (PSPGenesis and SNES9XTYL for Sega Genesis and Super Nintendo, for example), and a image of the PSP on the right that also displays the emulator title as you cycle through your options.

NesterJ

GAMES

> **TIP** When launching eLoader as above, make sure to wait a few seconds for all of the photos in your Photo menu to load completely. Otherwise, your PSP may lock up. If this happens, don't worry. You can always force it to shut down by holding the power slide up for ten seconds. Start the PSP up again, and all should be well.

At first, there may be a couple of screens that quickly flash some text before your game starts up – your emulator is running some system checks. We promise, nothing bad is happening. After a moment, your game will load, and you can play away!

To exit your game, you'll need to press the left shoulder button, left on the directional pad, or left on the analog stick, depending on which emulator you're running. Some emulators have an option in their menu to "exit emulator" – this will take you back to the eLoader screen, and from there you can press the Start button to return to the PSP menu. If there's no such option, hold down the left and right shoulder buttons along with the Start button for about a second. This will also take you back to the eLoader screen, and again, you can press Start to quit.

Versions 2.01 through 2.60

With versions 2.01 and upwards, Sony patched the exploit that lets you launch eLoader through the Photo menu. The developers of eLoader found another ingenious hole, though, using the game Grand Theft Auto: Liberty City Stories. If you're running version 2.01 or higher of the firmware, you need a copy of this game in order to run homebrew.

eLoader runs exactly as described above for version 2.00, but you won't be able to launch it through the Photo menu. Instead, set up eLoader as described on p.56. Launch GTA: Liberty City Stories, go to the **Load Game** option, and select eLoader. Once it's loaded, it runs just as it does in version 2.00, and will recognize files in the Game folder of your Memory Stick. Select an emulator, launch it, and you're on your way.

Version 2.70

Version 2.70 closed the GTA exploit that eLoader had been able to use. At press time, there was no way to run emulators on 2.70, but you can be sure that homebrew developers are working on it. Check the major PSP sites for the most recent developments.

WARNING! Not all homebrew games and applications will run through eLoader. Visit **www.noobz.eu** for the most up-to-date list of what homebrew will work with your version of eLoader.

Where do I find game ROMs?

Torrent sites are your best bet. ROMs can also be found in some game forums, on newsgroups, and even on some websites (although these sites tend to get shut down pretty quickly). You can even find complete sets of all games for a system – all NES games, for example – zipped into one download.

THE PSONE ON YOUR PSP

Sony is scheduled to launch what is surely the most powerful emulator for the PSP – or something like it, anyway. Towards the end of 2006, Sony will introduce a service through which you can download games for the first PlayStation (commonly referred to now as PSOne) to play on your PSP. At press time, few details were available, but PlayStation aficionados will surely appreciate this service – and the possibility of playing games like Metal Gear Solid and Final Fantasy VII on their commutes to work.

ELOADER

If you have an old PSP running version 1.50 firmware, it's easy to run homebrew and emulators;
if you have version 2.00, you can downgrade to run 1.50 (see
p.115). But what if you have a later version of firmware? Access to
homebrew and emulators isn't necessarily restricted to those who
bought their PSP early on, or have managed to get hold of a used
one. Hackers are a crafty bunch, and almost as soon as firmware
version 2.00 was released, a couple of individuals known as Fanjita
and Ditlew created a program called eLoader, and have successfully adapted it for every firmware update through version 2.60.

> **TIP** Visit **www.noobz.eu** to download eLoader and to check what home-
> brew is currently supported.

eLoader runs through certain holes in either firmware or game
software that are called exploits. For PSPs running version 2.00 of
the firmware, eLoader runs through an exploit in the PSP's Photo
menu. PSPs running version 2.01 or later run eLoader through an
exploit in the save function of the UMD game Grand Theft Auto:
Liberty City Stories. If your PSP has one of these more recent
versions of firmware, you can't run eLoader without GTA, and
before you install eLoader you will have to play and save at least
one GTA game.

> **TIP** Before you do any file swapping, always back up your Memory Stick
> by copying its contents onto your computer. If anything goes awry, you'll
> be able to restore all your data and game saves.

eLoader works by giving you a group of files to synchronize
with the files already on your PSP's Memory Stick. It's pretty
simple really, especially if you're running Windows – run the
Windows Installer that came with your download of eLoader.

Hook up your PSP to your PC, run the installer, and you're done. For Mac users, it's a little more complicated.

Installing eLoader on a Mac

To install eLoader onto a Mac, you'll have to manually input files and folders into different areas of your Memory Stick. Fortunately, the eLoader download comes with a readme.txt file that includes a complete list of files and folder pathways, which you can use as a checklist to make sure you've put all your downloaded files in the right place.

Upon opening the eLoader folder you'll notice that the folders it contains parallel those you have on your Memory Stick. You must not overwrite the PSP's folders, but instead take all the files from within the eLoader folder of the same name, and move them to the one on the Memory Stick. Within the PSP folder there will also be some subfolders that have the same names – again, **do not overwrite** one folder with another. For example (in the figure), inside the eLoader's PSP folder is a Photo folder. Take the files from inside the eLoader ▶ PSP ▶ Photo folder, and move them to Stan ▶ PSP ▶ Photo.

Before you go on, you'll need to update the saved game data. GTA will always load the latest saved game first, and since this is now technically eLoader, you'll need to reinstate an actual saved GTA game to set everything right. Updating is easily done if you you've backed up your game saves with a program like iPSP or Sony's PSP Media

Our manual install on a Mac. Note the top level files in eLoader (like 1_097.bin) are top level files in STAN.

Manager (see p.120) – just copy your latest game save from your computer back to your Memory Stick and your game will start normally.

If you don't use a media manager for your PSP, you'll need to reset your game save data manually.

58

1. First, copy your GTA saved game to your computer. You'll find a GTA saved game in PSP ▶ savedata ▶ ULUS10041S0 (see pic). Then delete the file from the Memory Stick.

2. Now take the version you saved on your computer, and copy it back to the Memory Stick in the same place you originally found it. This process gives your GTA game save a more recent time-stamp than the eLoader file.

Now disconnect your PSP from your computer and restart it. Once it's back up and running, make sure the GTA UMD is inserted and proceed as if you were about to play the game. The game will load and you'll find GTA's character, Tony, standing at your save spot. From here navigate to **Load Game**, where you'll find eLoader taking up a save slot – it will load itself in about 15 seconds once you've passed the "stop your previous game" query. Once up, eLoader will display a list of all the recognizable files within your game folder. For more on emulators and ROMs, see p.49. For more on homebrew applications, turn to the Firmware, Software, & Homebrew section (p.109).

> **WARNING!** Not all homebrew games and applications will run through eLoader. Visit **www.noobz.eu** for the most up-to-date list of what homebrew will work with your version of eLoader.

OLD FIRMWARE, NEW GAMES

The homebrew community has been frustrated by Sony's insistence that you upgrade your firmware to play new games. Many people want the best of both worlds – homebrew games *and* new games – without resorting to the two-PSP solution. Thus, a major strand of homebrew development has focused on finding a way to run games that require the latest version of firmware, but without having to update from version 1.50.

This development has met with mixed success. The first attempt was made by a group called MPH, whose MPH Game Loader was designed mostly to allow users of firmware version 1.50 to play GTA without upgrading to firmware version 2.00. It's rather complicated, and while for some it's worked like a charm, others have encountered problems trying to get it to work, especially with games besides GTA.

Basically an updated version of MPH Game Loader, **Run UMD** functions with a wider array of video games. It's generally restricted to running games that require firmware version 2.00, though, and newer games would not, at the time of writing, work with it.

The most recent program to address the problem is Genesis UMD Launcher 2.6, which true to its name is designed to launch UMDs that require you to upgrade to version 2.6 of the firmware.

Please note that these programs will work only if you're running version 1.50 of the PSP firmware. Just as importantly, be warned that they don't always work – some games will run, but others won't. As new games (and new versions of these programs)

GAMES

continue to be released, check out the PSP discussion boards (see p.177) for feedback before you install anything.

MPH Game Loader **mphwebsite.tuxfamily.org**
Run UMD **www.psp-hacks.com**
Genesis UMD Launcher 2.6 **www.projectpsp.com**

VIDEO, AUDIO
& PHOTOS

△

□ ○

✕

09

Video

movies, TV, home video

The PSP is capable of playing surprisingly high-quality video. According to Sony's specs, its 4.3-inch (10.9cm) widescreen display offers up to 16.77 million colors. And it has to be said, the video can be very impressive – it's crisp, and near-DVD quality – but for DVD-quality sound, you'll need some good headphones. In this section, we walk you through everything from watching a UMD film, to converting your DVDs to PSP-playable formats, to where you can find PSP-optimized video on the Internet. Digital video has been slower than digital music to catch on with consumers, but as broadband Internet access, higher file transfer speeds, and intuitive (and free) video software have become more widespread, manipulating digital video – and preparing it for your PSP – has become easier than ever.

UMD MOVIES

Watching films off UMD is a breeze. All you have to do is pop in a UMD movie, navigate to it through the **Video** menu, press the X button, and you get a menu screen just like with a DVD. Unlike DVDs, though, UMDs don't have lots of extra features – due to their small physical size and the limitations of optical storage, the amount of data a UMD can hold is limited. 1.8GB is still a lot of video, but to keep both video and audio quality up to par, the movie itself consumes most of the disc.

There are definite advantages to watching movies on UMD over watching them off the Memory Stick. Firstly, only the UMD format can fully exploit the resolution and quality of the PSP's video output. Plus, the PSP can be finicky about playing video off the Memory Stick (see p.69). But if you buy a UMD, it's pretty much guaranteed to work, barring any defect. Hundreds of movies, generally from the major studios and film distributors, are available in the format. You can even rent them online from Blockbuster Video in the US and from lovefilm.com in the UK.

Now for the downside. The list price for UMDs in the US ranges from twenty to thirty dollars, and in the UK from fifteen to twenty-five quid. That's expensive – generally, quite a bit more expensive than a DVD, and it's a less versatile format. You can't take a UMD to a friend's house to watch unless she has a PSP. Of course, you can bring your PSP, but what if you leave it on the bus or get it stolen? Losing a PSP is much more costly than losing a DVD. Also, the PSP is clearly a one-person device – sharing a screen isn't so hot, although you can, with moderate difficulty, hook the PSP up to your TV (see p.137).

AREN'T STUDIOS ABANDONING THE FORMAT?

It's hard to hit the right note when you manufacture a proprietary format. Sony took a pretty big gamble with UMD movies. Unlike DVD and VHS films, which can be watched on a wide variety of machines and screens, UMDs can only be watched on the Sony PSP. And while the quality of UMD films is very high, and they're sometimes advertised side by side with rabidly consumed DVDs, consumers aren't buying all that many of them. In early 2006, according to the *Hollywood Reporter*, a number of major movie studios drastically scaled back their release plans for the format, and Wal-Mart, America's largest retailer, reduced the shelf space reserved for UMD films. Given the millions of PSP users worldwide, it's unlikely that the UMD movie format will be completely abandoned. But since it's possible to convert your already purchased DVDs into PSP-viewable files (see below), it's not unreasonable to assume that many people will choose to go that route instead.

Backing up UMD movies

As we discussed in the Games section (see p.46), programs like Fast Loader allow you to copy UMD movies in pretty much the same way you copy UMD games. It's available for download at **www.psp-hacks.com**, as well as on a number of torrent sites. Now, if you own a UMD movie, why you'd be copying it is a bit beyond us, as it's kind of a pain. And while US copyright law has been interpreted by some lawyers as allowing consumers to have a single backup copy of any digital item, actually making that backup may not be legal in the US or elsewhere: signatories to the World Intellectual Property Organization Copyright Treaty are required to make illegal the circumvention of copy protection. So can you make a copy of something you're allowed to have? How can you be allowed to have a copy of something you can't make (or even buy)? This dilemma remains unresolved.

While doing some of what we discuss in this book might take you into legal gray areas, we must say that we don't condone distributing copied UMDs. Copying your film because the UMD is liable to accidental destruction, sure. Then you have a copy of something that you've paid good money for, and can still watch your movie if your dog eats your UMD.

MOVIES ON YOUR MEMORY STICK

Whatever happens to the UMD film format, it's still possible – and just as easy – to watch movies (and other video content) on your PSP using the Memory Stick. Simply navigate to the Memory Stick icon in the PSP's **Video** menu, select it, and you'll see any video files you have stored on the Memory Stick. Since the cost of 1GB and 2GB Memory Sticks has dropped from obscene to merely high, putting a couple of movies on your Memory Stick for an airplane trip is within the realm of the affordable.

While playing movies off the Memory Stick is easy, getting those video files properly formatted and properly placed can be quite tricky. As is the case with music, photos, and any games not on UMDs, you'll need to hook up to a computer with a USB connection to get this all set up (see p.7).

How do I get movies onto the Memory Stick?

The PSP doesn't come with a program that lets you sync it with your computer. This is less of a problem for photo, audio, and game content – when you format your Memory Stick on your PSP, it creates clearly labeled folders for all of these media. Video is another matter. The Memory Stick doesn't have a "Movies" folder; instead, its video folders are hidden away inside the **MP_ROOT** folder (see p.72). And on top of that, the PSP is very, very finicky about video formats. Not only must your video files be in MP4

VIDEO, AUDIO & PHOTOS

or AVC format, they also have a cap on resolution, and a peculiar naming convention that you absolutely must follow.

MPEG-4

Brought to us by the same people who delivered the popular MP3 audio format, MPEG-4 actually encompasses a fairly wide set of digital content, from the AAC audio files you download from Apple's iTunes Store to the video files you create from your own DVDs. It's actually a set of standards that tells programmers how to encode content, and your computer or digital media device how to decode it. Most relevant to video for the PSP are parts 2 and 10 of the standards, commonly called MP4 and AVC respectively. We use this shorthand throughout the rest of this section, and you'll generally see the same terms used when you're downloading video from the Internet.

MP4 was the first type of video file handled by the PSP and it has certain advantages, namely being able to support high resolution – much higher resolution than you need for the PSP. For example, MP4 files allow for reasonably good quality should you hook a video iPod up to a television – something that the PSP can't natively do (see p.137). Also, MP4 is the only format that firmware versions 1.50, 1.51, and 1.52 support (see pp.112-113).

AVC stands for Advanced Video Coding and, true to its name, it supports higher video quality per megabyte. If, for example, you were to convert *Spiderman 2* into both MP4 and AVC, and both versions took up the same amount of memory, the AVC version would be of a noticeably higher quality.

You should feel free to use whichever format suits you best, but overall, we recommend AVC for the PSP – it gives you better video in fewer megabytes, and getting the most bang for your memory buck is vital when it comes to maximizing the video potential of your Memory Stick.

There are a number of different methods of converting and transferring video to the PSP, but by far the simplest and most reliable is to use a media manager. Media managers automatically convert your video files into a PSP-viewable MP4 or AVC file, and they'll put the files in the correct folder on your Memory Stick as well. See p.120 for more on media manager software.

Can I convert my DVDs?

Yes, but it's a little tricky. Generally, you have to go through two processes – ripping your DVD to your computer, then converting the files you ripped into a PSP-viewable format. The legality of ripping DVDs for your own personal use is uncertain, but it's nevertheless easy enough to do.

DVDs are encoded with something called a Content Scrambling System (CSS), meaning that if you try to copy the video files you'll end up with nothing but a bunch of garbage data. However, a few years back a programmer named Jon Johansen (and two others who remain anonymous) caused a huge stir by releasing a small program called **DeCSS** that enabled users to successfully bypass CSS and extract video files from DVDs. Two very effective programs that do the same have been released since then, but all have been driven underground because of legal concerns. Nevertheless, you can still find them on file-sharing services and torrent sites. For Windows, a program called **DVD Decrypter** extracts files called Video Object files, or VOBs. For Mac, a program called **Mac the Ripper** does the same thing, but the files it extracts are in a "Video_TS" folder. These files and folders can then be used by a variety of programs to create PSP-viewable files.

While DVD Decrypter and Mac the Ripper can be difficult to find, there are other, more readily available programs that can convert your DVDs into usable files. In fact, one of the media managers we recommend (see p.123), iPSP (Windows and Mac), can convert DVDs directly into PSP-viewable format, which can save a fair amount of time – it even places them in the proper Memory Stick folder for you. Xilisoft has a Windows program called DVD to PSP Suite that helps you do the same thing, as does PQDVD's PSP Movie Creator (also for Windows). For Mac, there's a very handy program called Handbrake that copies DVDs to various video formats. Alternatively, you can use a stripped-down version of Handbrake designed specifically to output video for iPods and PSPs, called Instant Handbrake.

Remember, DVDs contain a huge amount of data. It's not like ripping a CD, which can take as little as a few minutes. Unless you have a very powerful computer, you can expect to spend about the same amount of time processing a film from a DVD as you would watching it.

DVD to PSP Suite www.xilisoft.com
PSP Movie Creator www.pqdvd.com/psp
Handbrake and Instant Handbrake handbrake.m0k.org

Naming your video files

Unfortunately, you can't name them things like "Super Troopers. MP4." The PSP has very peculiar and particular naming requirements.

MP4 files must be labeled in the following format: **M4Vxxxxx. MP4**. Each x stands for a number, and the file names can range from M4V00001.MP4 through M4V99999.MP4. Letters must be capitalized.

AVC files must be labeled in the following format: **MAQxxxxx. MP4**. Again, each x stands for a number, and the file names can range from MAQ00001.MP4 through MAQ99999.MP4. Letters must be capitalized.

TIP Don't fall prey to the temptation to rename your files something sensible, like "Baby First Steps.MP4" – your PSP simply won't play it.

So how can I tell what M4V00096.MP4 is?

Media managers and some other programs (such as Toast) will automatically create or help you select a thumbnail image to represent the movie in the PSP's **Video** menu. These images are small JPEG files that are labeled with the extension ".THM," and, thankfully, it's also possible to create them yourself. Pick any image you want to use, be it something you've grabbed from the video, a download of a movie poster, anything. Then all you need to do is use any photo editor that can save JPEG files, from iPhoto up to Photoshop. The JPEG needs to be saved at 160x120 size.

Take your saved JPEG and rename it to match your movie. For example, if your movie is saved as M4V54321.MP4, then your thumbnail file must be named M4V54321.THM. Drop the image file and the movie into the same folder in **MP_ROOT** as described on the next page, and you should see your custom thumbnail image when you go to the **Video** menu on the Memory Stick.

Manually formatting movies for the Memory Stick

At this point, if you've decided to use a media manager or video converter that lets you convert your DVDs or files directly into a PSP format before automatically dropping them into the right folder of the Memory Stick. If, however, you're using a program like ffmpegX or Roxio's Toast to create video files, you'll probably want a bit more technical info.

Frame Size, Bitrate, and Frame Rate

The technical details of formatting movies for the Memory Stick might seem a little complicated, but they're not beyond the skills of a moderately technically adept person. Frame Size, Bitrate, and Frame Rate are the parameters that determine both the quality as well as the final size of your video file. Only UMDs can display at 480x272, the full resolution of the PSP's screen. We recommend you play around a bit with resolution and bitrate if you're using a program, like Toast or Handbrake, that lets you manually adjust these levels. Some people report being able to squeeze out slightly higher resolution or sampling rates than those we detail below. First of all, though, you have to choose between formatting your movies as MP4 or AVC files.

MP4 files must have a resolution or frame size of 320x240 (for 4:3 screen proportion) or 368x208 (for 16:9 screen proportion). Supposedly a 2.35:1 ratio can be supported as well (416x176). Use whichever is closest to the original ratio of the source video for the best results. For your frame size, the multiple of your width by height cannot exceed 76,800. We understand that smaller sizes may work, but our attempts to run smaller sizes failed to a one. Any larger, and your MP4 almost certainly won't play on the PSP. The bitrate (the quality at which the video is sampled) should not exceed 768 kbps. This bitrate covers both video and audio, so the actual video bitrate should not exceed 640 kbps, allowing 128 kbps for sound. The frame rate (the number of frames per second displayed by the video) can be either 14.985 or 29.97 fps; the latter gives better quality.

AVC files have pretty much the same frame sizes – 320x240, 368x208, 416x176. Again, if the multiple of width by height exceeds 76,800, the AVC file won't play on the PSP. Believe us, we've tried. The bitrate for AVC video can be less than that of MP4 – anywhere between 10% to 30% less – and will keep the same quality. The frame rate should be the same as for MP4: 29.97 or 14.985 fps, with 29.97 delivering better quality.

Where do I put video files?

If you're not using a media manager, you'll have to transfer your video files manually. It's essential that these go into the proper directory, or the PSP won't be able to find them to play them. On your formatted Memory Stick you'll find a folder called MP_ ROOT, and inside it two subfolders: 100MNV01 and 100ANV01.

These, in fact, are the video folders for the PSP: **100MNV01** is for MP4 files, and **100ANV01** is for AVC files. However tempting it seems, don't rename these folders – if you do, the PSP won't recognize them as directories of video files, and then you won't be able to play anything. An easy way to remember which folder is for which files: MP4 goes in the folder with the letter M in its name; AVC goes in the folder with the letter A in its name.

TELEVISION FOR YOUR PSP

The PSP has neither an aerial nor a coaxial input, so the normal ways to access television programming are irrelevant. There are, however, a few ways to get your TV fix using your PSP.

TV from your Digital Video Recorder

Home digital recording devices (the DVR you get from your cable company or the PVR from companies like Sky) record pristine digital copies of your favorite TV shows. Where do you think all of those high-quality TV downloads you've been finding online "for free" are from, anyway?

The easiest way to watch TV using your PSP is to use Sony's Location Free Player (see p.158), which streams TV from your recorder to your PSP anywhere in the world you can find a WiFi connection.

Alternatively, if you're one of those clever people who know how to copy a TV show from your recorder and decode it into a viewable form, you can then convert the video file to a PSP-viewable format as we described earlier (p.70).

Finally, Sony manufactures HDD/DVD recorders (that is, video recorders that store shows on hard disk or record to DVD) that allow you to get video directly onto your PSP without the use of a computer. However, outside of Japan, these are not yet available through regular retail outlets. But there's always a chance that your favorite electronics importer might carry them – at a substantial premium, we're sure.

CAN I WATCH TV SHOWS FROM ITUNES ON THE PSP?

Sadly, it appears not. We've looked extensively for a software workaround that lets you convert your iTunes-purchased shows into a PSP-viewable format, but we haven't been able to find one. By the time this book is in your hand, it may well be possible – as always, we suggest you poke around online to find out.

Can I use my Slingbox with my PSP?

Not at the moment. Sony has declined to interface the PSP with the Slingbox, a system that allows you to stream your home TV to wherever you are via the Internet, probably because they offer a competing product with the Location Free Player. This, however, wouldn't preclude the manufacturer of Slingbox from figuring out how to make the Slingbox and the PSP get along, but there's no word that anything like that is in the works. A solution isn't terribly likely to come out of the homebrew community – hacking two well-protected proprietary machines and integrating them is a hefty project.

WHERE CAN I DOWNLOAD PSP VIDEOS?

A number of websites offer PSP-optimized video for download. Some sites we've come across are:

PSP Set www.pspset.com
Some cartoon shorts, music videos, and trailers (including old Superman Cartoons!).

Sony Connect psp.connect.com
Official content for the PSP from Sony – like other Sony products, this is for Windows only.

Pocket Movies www.pocketmovies.net
A variety of animated shorts.

GameSpot www.gamespot.com/features/pspresourcecenter/
Downloadable video game reviews and trailers.

Men's magazine FHM www.fhm.com/site/psp/main.asp
Offers its typically racy content – video from photo shoots and the like, as well as a couple of interviews.

The 29 Network www.29hdnetwork.com/29MP4VS/index.html
A handful of feature films, formatted for the PSP, for $2.99 each.

Fuse www.fusetv.com
Music TV network site with PSP-viewable downloads of interviews with a variety of musicians and bands.

Atom Films www.atomfilms.com/af/togo/
An assortment of free short films formatted for the PSP.

Google Video video.google.com
Offers both free and purchased content for the PSP.

10

Audio

music, audiobooks, podcasts

Since the advent of the MP3 file format, the distribution of music has been steadily shifting towards the digital realm. In 2006, Apple's iTunes store sold its one billionth song, and the amount of music sold online continues to accelerate – a track reached number one in the UK music charts even before it was released on CD. Getting music without leaving your computer is easier than ever – and audiobooks, streaming radio, and podcasts are all just a mouse-click away as well. And anything that's just a mouse-click away is just about ready for the PSP.

MUSIC ON THE PSP

Regardless of where you get your music from, the PSP lets you take it with you wherever you go, via the Memory Stick. The PSP manual is fairly clear about how to actually navigate music folders and play music files once they're on your PSP, be it with the PSP controls or the remote, so we're going to concentrate here on more complex issues – file conversion, and the various ways of getting your digital music collection onto the Memory Stick.

MUSIC ONLINE

In addition to iTunes, MSN, Yahoo!, Rhapsody, the reborn Napster, eMusic. com, mp3.com, and countless other sites sell digital music online, whereas free MP3 downloads are available from a number of sites, such as the love-to-hate-it indie site Pitchforkmedia.com, music.download.com, the online edition of *Vice* magazine, epitonic.com, and others – enough to fill your MP3 player many times over. What's more, bands often offer a handful of MP3 files through their websites. Of course, innumerable MP3 tracks are available over the (in)famous peer-to-peer networks like Limewire, Morpheus, and Grokster, as well as through the various torrent sites like Pirate Bay and Torrentbox.com. For more on all of this, check out the *Rough Guide to iPods, iTunes & Music Online*.

Converting audio files

Numerous media players for Windows and OSX let you convert your CDs into PSP-supported formats. Windows Media Player, iTunes, and Real Player are just a few that allow you to easily create MP3 files. You're probably already using one if you listen to CDs on your computer. There are other, more rare types of digital music that can be found online – Ogg Vorbis is one of the larger ones. Numerous programs can convert other types of file to MP3 or unprotected AAC – do a search online for "converting [file type X] to [file type Y]," and you'll find a slew of options, including

VIDEO, AUDIO & PHOTOS

some freeware that works quite well. We like Switch (**nch.com.au/ switch**) for Windows or Mac, and Audion (**www.panic.com/audion**) for Mac.

FILE FORMATS

The PSP supports the following types of audio file:

ATRAC3, ATRAC3plus Sony's proprietary audio format, almost exclusively seen when buying music from Sony's Connect music store.

MP3 The Golden Oldie of compressed digital audio.

MP4 (aka AAC, .m4a, .m4p) AAC is the compressed audio format that iTunes encodes, unless you set it to do otherwise.

WAV (aka Linear PCM) Uncompressed digital audio files. They're very large, so they aren't terribly suitable for a digital music player or your PSP.

WMA (aka Windows Media Audio): The format used, generally, by Windows Media Player. In relative terms, WMA encoding is not that widespread, but many people do use it – especially if they use a digital music player other than the iPod. Some online music stores, like HMV's online store in the UK, also use the format.

TIP If you use iTunes, your unprotected AAC files might have the file extension .m4a. The PSP won't play files with the .m4a extension, but luckily, all you have to do is rename the file with the extension .aac, and you'll be able to play the track.

77

MUSIC UMDS

So far, at least, UMD remains a video format. As far as we can tell, most of what's offered as "UMD Music" is either live concert video (which you can listen to with or without the screen turned on, of course) or "making of" documentaries about classic albums like Nirvana's "Nevermind" or Pink Floyd's "Dark Side of the Moon" (which don't actually include the album itself, although there's surely enough space on the UMD for it).

TIP Not all versions of firmware support all audio formats. Check out the firmware chart on pp.112–113.

Copy protection

Copy protection is commonly found on digital music purchased from an online music seller – Sony's Connect store has it, as does iTunes, Napster, and others. The PSP's ability to play copy-protected files is limited. Much the same way that songs bought on iTunes can be played on iPods but no other MP3 players, songs bought from Connect can only be played on Sony devices – and the PSP therefore supports the ATRAC format (these files have .omg, .oma, or .atp file extensions), and only that format. Copy-protected WMA files won't work, nor will the protected AAC files that Apple sells through the iTunes store (these have the file extension .m4p).

Now, combating copy protection is a favorite activity of programmers worldwide, so there are a number of programs that allow you to convert copy-protected files into MP3s, including Tunebite (for both copy-protected WMA and AAC files – **www.tunebite.com**) and the Hymn Project (for copy-protected AAC files – **www.hymn-project.org**). Additionally, programs that allow you to record in real time, such as high-end editing software like ProTools or Logic, as well as the eminently affordable Audio Hijack Pro (Mac only, $32, www.rogueamoeba.com), can easily copy protected files. But there's another workaround that's extremely simple and totally free. When you burn regular audio CDs from copy-protected digital files (usually by selecting "Burn CD" or "Export" from the file menus for most media players), it seems to strip them of their copy protection as it makes the CD playable for your stereo. You can then put the CD back in your computer, convert those tracks back to MP3 or unprotected AAC files, and then play them on your PSP. If you use a CD-RW, you could repeat the process indefinitely using only the one disc. Not the most elegant of solutions, it's true, but it does get those songs you own only as copy-protected audio files onto your PSP.

Organizing your music files

The PSP does not automatically synchronize with your computer the way the iPod does with iTunes, but manual transfer is thankfully very straightforward. When you formatted your Memory Stick (p.32), one of the folders created in the process was **Music**. Connect the PSP to your computer with the USB, then all you need to do in both Windows XP and Mac OSX is select which songs you'd like to hear, and drag the files into the Music folder.

TIP If you use a Sony VAIO computer, you can just plug the Memory Stick into the appropriate port. If you're using a USB Memory Stick reader/writer, you can plug the Memory Stick into that. Don't forget to follow normal insertion and removal procedures to avoid corrupting data.

The Memory Stick's file architecture is not that complex, and the Music folder is therefore fairly restricted. If you've already dropped audio files into the Music folder, you'll see that they have (more or less, anyway) the same names that you have for them on your computer. But they're not organized in any particular way.

The way around this disorder is to make use of what the PSP manual calls "Group Mode." A **Group** in the Music folder of the PSP is simply a subfolder that contains audio files. So if, for example, you have a folder on your computer called "Public Enemy – Fear of a Black Planet," inside of which are the MP3 files of the songs from that album, you can copy that folder to the PSP's Music folder. When you navigate to the Memory Stick under the Music menu, you'll see a Group designated by a white square (if you don't have the cover art file) or by the album cover (if you do). It'll tell you how many tracks are in that group, and you'll be able to play only that group should you desire to play just that album.

When putting groups of songs onto the Memory Stick, make sure that there are no subfolders within the groups. For example, we have two (legal) Miles Davis albums saved in iTunes – *A Tribute to Jack Johnson* and *Doo-Bop*. Now, if we were to copy our Miles Davis folder from our iTunes library right onto the Memory Stick, we'd see this:

However, if we put the albums in separately, we see this:

Each album shows us the number of tracks, which we can now access. If your computer's music management program groups your music by artist then by album (as iTunes does), then you may want to rename the album folders to include the artist name when you put them on the Memory Stick, in order to find them more easily.

OTHER TYPES OF AUDIO

Audiobooks

Audiobooks are readily available on CD, and are also sold as copy-protected digital files on sites like **www.audible.com** and Apple's iTunes store. With CDs, you can convert them to MP3 files just as you can with songs. Since they're usually only spoken audio, you can often save them at a lower bitrate, thus cramming more audiobook content per megabyte than you'd want to with songs.

In order to get copy-protected downloaded files on your PSP, you'll have to convert them to an unprotected format using a program like Tunebite (see p.78). It's not a good idea to burn to a CD and then convert back like you might with a music CD – audiobooks can take up many discs, and you'd ultimately spend more on blank media than you would on software to do it for you.

DELETING MUSIC FILES

For some reason, deleting music from the Memory Stick doesn't always free up the memory used by the file. It's pretty easy to get that memory back, though. Simply back up the data you'd like to save from the Memory Stick as detailed on p.33. Then format your Memory Stick again through the **Settings** menu. Once you've done that, add any folders or files back onto the Memory Stick that you'd like to restore, and you're good to go.

This seems to happen more frequently when deleting files from the Memory Stick using the computer. If you delete files or groups using the PSP itself (through the options menu), the space seems to become immediately available, although if there's other data in a group (such as cover art), the PSP will delete the music files, but not the group itself – you'll need to do that through the computer.

Podcasts

Podcasts, as audio RSS feeds are known, have become something of a phenomenon: the free podcast produced by Ricky Gervais (of "The Office" fame) became so popular – generating 4 million downloads – that they started charging for it. And podcasts' popularity for both creators and consumers is still on the rise. Everybody from National Public Radio and the BBC to your local newspaper to hobbyists with a microphones and Apple's GarageBand is making podcasts. They're (almost always) free, and that means you can get to hear radio programs you enjoy without having to tune in to a radio at a specific time. If you're interested in exploring the world of podcasts, you can investigate them at the websites of most major news organizations as well as aggregator sites like **www.podcastalley.com**. Of course, the omnipresent iTunes offers free podcasts as well.

If you already download podcasts to your computer, you're probably getting them as MP3 files. Just like with songs, you can drop these in the Music folder of your Memory Stick and play away. With the release of version 2.70 of the firmware, the PSP became able to both stream podcasts and download them directly. See p.106 in the Networking section for details.

MEDIA MANAGERS

While manual transfer is pretty easy, moving stuff around with a media manager can be even easier. Media managers are programs that index audio, video, photo, or game content for your PSP – or sometimes all of them. While iTunes and your PSP won't normally get along, there are a number of programs designed specifically to handle your PSP's organizational needs when it comes to media. We address media managers more thoroughly in the Software section (see p.120).

Photos

pictures, slideshows, wallpaper

Videos might be a pain, and music isn't so bad, but by far the easiest form of your own content to use on the PSP is digital photos. The PSP can display a variety of common photo formats; you need not optimize their size before dropping them on the Memory Stick, as with video; and you can use the same Memory Stick PRO Duo with certain Sony cameras and the PSP. It's also very easy to view your pictures as a slideshow, use a photo to create custom wallpaper, or send a photo to your friend's PSP.

GETTING PHOTOS ONTO YOUR PSP

Image formats

The PSP supports the following photo formats: JPEG (.jpg extension), TIFF (.tif extension), GIF (.gif extension), PNG (.png extension), and BMP (.bmp extension). Of these JPEG is probably the most common format – if you use a standard consumer digital camera, you probably save your photos as JPEGs already

– with TIFF coming second. Suffice to say that the vast majority of photo files you'll take with your camera, receive from friends, or download from the Internet will already be a file type that the PSP can display.

These image types are all part of the group known as bitmap images. All this means is that these file types have a fixed resolution of pixels set in a grid. When you change a bitmap image, to enlarge or shrink it for example, your editing software does something called resampling – reviewing the original image to see how best to convert it into your new format.

In contrast, if you use a program like Adobe Illustrator to create your own image (for example, some kind of custom background for your PSP), you'll make what's known as a vector image – an image that you can resize without having to resample it. Vector types aren't supported by the PSP, so if you're using them, you'll have to save them as one of the bitmap file types mentioned above in order to use them.

SONY CAMERAS AND THE MEMORY STICK

If you own a Sony digital camera that takes the Memory Stick Duo or Memory Stick PRO Duo, you can use your PSP's Memory Stick directly in the camera. In the PSP's **Photo** menu, you'll see a folder that you won't see on your computer – it's called Digital Camera Images. When using your Memory Stick with a Sony camera, this is usually where your photos will be saved. Sometimes, a camera will also let you choose which folder to save to, and in that case, you can place photos you take in any Memory Stick folder that your camera can read. We recommend using the Photos folder and its subfolders – otherwise the PSP probably won't be able to locate your picture later on.

Transferring the files

If you've formatted your Memory Stick, it will have a Photos folder ready and waiting. All you need to do is connect with your computer and drag and drop the photos you want into this folder. If you already have photos saved in a folder on your computer, or if you create folders to organize your pictures from special events (like "Nick's Wedding" or "Sean's Bris"), you can just drag and drop those folders as well.

You can also use a media manager to organize your photos and move them to the PSP – see p.120 for our discussion of media manager programs and their features.

VIEWING PHOTOS

Creating a PSP slideshow

Putting together a slideshow is remarkably simple. Group whatever images you'd like to include in your slideshow into one folder on the Memory Stick. Navigate to the **Photo** menu, select the folder, and press the triangle button – a menu will pop up that includes a **Slideshow** option. Select that and the PSP goes into slideshow mode – you can toggle between images in the slideshow by pressing the left or right shoulder buttons. To change the slideshow speed, go into **Settings ▸ Photo Settings** and select Slow, Normal, or Fast.

Creating custom PSP wallpaper

You'll need to use photo editing software on your computer to best create custom wallpaper. To make sure your photo fills the screen, crop your photos to a 16:9 width:height ratio – you can do this using your software's "constraint" feature or by customsizing your photo. Size the photo at 420x270 resolution or higher, maintaining the 16:9 ratio, and drop it into the PSP's Photo folder. Navigate to the picture you want, press triangle to get into the photo options menu, select "set as wallpaper," and say yes to overwrite the existing wallpaper.

Sharing photos with another PSP

The ability to share photos with other PSP users is conveniently built in to the PSP. If you and a friend are in the same room, you can send your photos to her, using the **Image Transfer** feature of the Photo menu. Go to the picture you want to send, but don't press X to display it; instead, while you have the cursor on the picture, press the triangle button. Make sure your WLAN switch is turned on, select "Send," and your PSP will look for other PSPs to send to. The nickname of your friend's PSP should pop up, and if she goes to the "Receive" option in her Photo menu, she can download your photo.

NETWORKING

△
□
○
✕

12

Wireless networks

Infrastructure and Ad Hoc modes

Not so long ago mobile phones were the size of toasters, PDAs were paper planners, and computers were tethered to telephone cables. But with the advent of WiFi – a means of sending files from computer to computer over radio waves – those dusty tangled cables are on the verge of extinction. In fact, almost every "portable" computing device made in the last couple of years comes with built-in WiFi capabilities, and the PSP is no exception. You can use the PSP's WiFi for multiplayer gaming (see p.45), for browsing the Web (see p.98), and for uploading and downloading files (see p.101), but before diving in you'll need to tinker with a few network settings.

Chapter 12

What you'll need

The PSP is capable of wireless multiplayer game play without an Internet connection, but if you want to browse the Web or play games online, you need more than just your shiny new friend – you need access to a wireless network, and quite possibly a password. If you've set up your own wireless network at home, you'll already have all the equipment, password, and settings information you need for a quick connection, but when you're out and about you may encounter some very different types of wireless network. Fortunately, the Easy network setup (see "quick start" on the next page) should work most of the time, but for unwieldy networks you have many customizable options at your command (see p.96).

WHAT IS WIFI?

WiFi is a label slapped on devices like routers and computers that are capable of broadcasting and receiving data over high-frequency radio waves. The term is also used to describe wireless networks in general – such as Google's city-spanning WiFi network planned for San Francisco, or Sony's planned WiFi "hotspots" distributed throughout the European continent. Most computers made today are shipped "WiFi enabled," and, depending on the specific wireless standard informing the hardware design, are able to transmit data at increasingly speedy rates. For instance, the PSP operates something called the 802.11b standard, meaning it can transfer information at a maximum rate of 11Mbits/sec (the same as most laptops). But there are newer and faster standards, such as 802.11g and the still theoretical 802.11n. It is rumored that there is actually an 802.11g enabled chip in the PSP, although you won't find it on tech specs anywhere.

NETWORK SETTINGS

First things first – slide the Wireless Local Area Network (WLAN) switch on the left side of the PSP upward. Turning on the WLAN switch tells the PSP to wake up its WiFi card and get ready to interact with other PSPs and your network. Then, from the main menu, head to **Settings** ▸ **Network Settings** and you're presented with two options: Ad Hoc Mode and Infrastructure Mode.

> **TIP** Head directly to the www icon and, provided you haven't already created one, you'll be prompted to make an Internet connection for Infrastructure Mode (see below).

Ad Hoc Mode

The more simple of the networking choices is Ad Hoc Mode – an extremely local (approximately 20–30ft or 10m) networking arrangement that lets your PSP "talk" to as many as 16 other PSPs without using the Internet as an intermediary. On the Ad Hoc settings screen you'll see the option of selecting one of three channels, plus an **Automatic** setting, which is nearly foolproof. If you find yourself in a room with more than just your own multiplayer battle, you'll have to agree among yourselves who gets channel 1, 6, or 11. For more on Ad Hoc game play, see p.45.

Infrastructure Mode – quick start

You'll end up interacting with the Infrastructure Mode settings way more than the Ad Hoc options, because as you move from one wireless zone to the next, you'll have to set up new, dedicated connections. Fortunately, the setup process is simple and clear, and most of it is automated, meaning you won't need to involve yourself with custom options like static IPs and proxy settings unless you really want to (see pp.96-97).

Upon selecting **New Connection**, you'll be asked to give it a name. You can save up to ten different wireless connections, so when concocting a title choose something that will represent the location of each wireless network (e.g. Home, Dad's house, Bateman's place). With the name set, select **Scan** and the PSP will search the surrounding area for all available wireless networks. Choose the one that belongs to you, enter your password if the network is secure, and select **Easy** to let your PSP and the network sort out all of the connection details automatically. That's pretty much it. Test your connection to make sure it works, and you're ready to cruise the Web or lead a team through a SOCOM mission.

If you ever need to make changes to your settings, like revising the name of a network connection from Starbucks to Fivebucks, highlight the connection on your Network Settings screen, and press the triangle button to reveal a sidebar of editing options.

Network Settings		WLAN Settings

Select the access point to be used.

SSID	Security	Signal Strength
EURONY	None	90%
thegroove	WEP	52%
tsunami	None	27%
osmosis	WEP	22%

✗ Enter   ⭘ Back

TIP You can get slightly faster download speeds if you turn off the **WLAN Power Save** feature in your **Power Save Settings**; just be sure to turn the WLAN switch off when you're not networking, as your WiFi card draws a standby charge and will suck up precious battery life waiting for networking instructions.

USE PROTECTION

Wireless routers can provide two kinds of security for their wireless networks: WEP (Wired Equivalent Privacy) and WPA (WiFi Protected Access). Both are simply ways of encrypting your data so random people can't swoop in and steal your files in transit, but WPA is the more secure of the two. The PSP can interact with either of these security protocols, ensuring network security compatibility for the foreseeable future. It even supports both flavors of WAP security: TKIP (Temporal Key Integrity Protocol) and AES (Advanced Encryption Standard).

The difference between the security types is subtle but significant. WEP was the first wireless security protocol, and has performed valiantly for a number of years. But very soon after it was released security experts discovered that by "listening" to enough transmissions from the same WEP encrypted network, they could translate the coding information and secretly enter the data stream. In response to this, encryption experts developed a method of disguising data with constantly changing codes known as temporal keys. While WEP-secured networks use the same coding for each transmission, every new stream of data sent over a WPA network has a unique encoding that is extremely difficult to crack. Of course, that extra encryption doesn't come without a price – in this case, slower Internet speeds. Luckily, WPA comes in two types, with the streamlined AES version using far fewer system resources for its encryption process, meaning quicker Web surfing and file downloads for you.

Infrastructure Mode – Customized

Sometimes you're on an old network and the easy method won't work, or maybe you want to tweak the network settings to conform to some particular specifications. While it's nice when networks agree to exchange information automatically, the PSP is also clever enough to deal with a crotchety network that demands manual attention. At the **IP Address** screen, click on **Custom** and through a series of pages you're given the chance to manipulate the following settings.

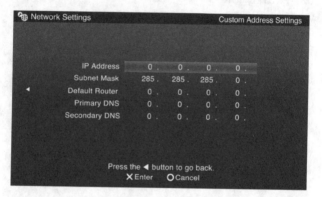

IP Address	0 .	0 .	0 .	0 .
Subnet Mask	285 .	285 .	285 .	0 .
Default Router	0 .	0 .	0 .	0 .
Primary DNS	0 .	0 .	0 .	0 .
Secondary DNS	0 .	0 .	0 .	0 .

Network Settings — Custom Address Settings

Press the ◀ button to go back.
✕ Enter   ◯ Cancel

You can handle just about all your manual entries on this one screen.

▶ **IP Address Setting** You will have to enter an IP address into your PSP if you are connecting to a network server that issues static IP address (a tedious and nearly extinct process).

▶ **PPPoE** If you use DSL for your high-speed Internet connection and you don't use a router, you may have to enter a PPPoE username and password. This is increasingly rare.

- **DNS Setting** If you'd like to use a specific Domain Name Server to initiate Web searches, enter its address here. It's useful to know where this is if you use the Wipeout Pure hack to go online (see p.100).

- **Proxy Server** If you use a proxy server to mask your IP address, enter its address here and set the port number to match the channel your router is comfortable with – it will likely find it by default.

TIP If you ever need to manually enter the PSP's MAC address, it can be found in **Settings** ▶ **System Settings** ▶ **System Information**.

NETWORKING

13

Surfing the Web

The PSP Internet Browser

One of the best things about the PSP's 2.00 firmware upgrade
(see p.110) was the addition of an Internet Browser. The browser
may not be able to handle streaming music or video, but the latest
version offers limited support for RSS feeds, and you do get a lot
of the functionality found in full-fledged web browsers like Safari
or Explorer. You can scroll through pages, write in text fields,
adjust the screen to your liking, save files, and perform other
functions we'll discuss throughout the chapter.

NAVIGATING THE PAGE

Make your way to the www icon www on the Home menu to launch the Internet Browser and load your homepage (by default this will be gray nothingness; see p.104 for homepage settings). You can use the D-pad to highlight text fields and Web links, or use the analog stick like a mouse to move your pointer all around the page. If the site you're on extends beyond the screen's frame (most websites are designed for full-sized computer monitors, so they won't fit on the PSP's small screen), hold down the square button while using the D-pad or analog stick, and you'll scroll the page in that direction.

You can open up to three separate pages at once. Position your cursor over a link, and hold down the X button to open that website in a new tab. Switch tabs by holding the square button and pressing either of the shoulder buttons.

❶ = back

❷ = forward

❸ = change fields on page

❺ = move pointer

X = enter

△ = browser menu and address entry

□ + ❶ or ❷ = switch tab

□ + ❺ = scroll page

□ + ❸ = scroll through fields

You can password protect the Internet Browser under **Settings** ▶ **Security Settings** ▶ **Internet Browser**. You'll be asked for your current password (the default is 0000). To change the password, move up one level to **Change Password**, enter your current password, and then create a new one. The PSP will now ask for this code before launching the browser, keeping your online history safe from prying eyes.

WEB ACCESS FOR 1.5 FIRMWARE

Before Sony released their Internet Browser, crafty individuals had already figured out ways to get the PSP online. The most popular method combined a download feature in the game Wipeout Pure with a simple network settings adjustment. No matter your firmware version, Wipeout Pure can connect to a website containing game updates, but as it isn't a browser you can't move beyond that page. But by changing the DNS in your network settings (see p.97) you can access a website that will act as a portal onto the Internet.

In response to one of the many PSP hacker challenges that pop up throughout the year, a fellow named Roto developed and posted clear instructions for the so-called Wipeout browser. He's also included some examples of DNS addresses to try, and instructions on the much more advanced procedure of setting up your own web portal.

Roto's Wipeout Web Browser Trick
http://omlette.net/psp/roto/

BROWSER FUNCTIONS

The Internet Browser doesn't provide a stunning array of customizable features and shortcuts, but it does get the basics right. When viewing a webpage, press the triangle button to reveal the browser's menu (press triangle again to hide it). Shaded areas encroach upon the screen from top and bottom, presenting you with an address bar, Back and Forward arrows, a home page icon, Stop and Refresh buttons, and a History icon. There are also icons for File, Bookmarks, View, and Tools that take you to further levels of menu.

Behind the help feature is a quick reference screen showing all the navigation controls.

File: Saving files from downloads

The **File** menu option will let you enter an address, open a link in a new tab, provide some page information, and shut down the browser entirely. But perhaps its most useful feature is its file saving options.

File

TEXT FILES FOR THE PSP – USING THE INTERNET BROWSER TO STORE AND READ DOCUMENTS

The easiest way to convert and organize text files on the PSP is to use one of the PSP data management programs discussed in Chapter 15, but if you don't want to further burden your computer (and your wallet) with yet another program, you can convert and upload text files with just about any word processing program.

First, on your computer open the document you want to read on your PSP in Word or another word processing program. Then, with your PSP in USB mode and attached to your computer, use the word processor's save options to turn the document into a Web file (the file will take the extension .htm or .html). Save your new Web file to the PSP's **Browser** folder (found under **PSP** ▶ **System** ▶ **Browser**). If you want to make sure all your page formatting goes through properly, and it's an option presented to you, save the page in Unicode.

To find your saved files, open the browser, and instead of typing "http://" into the address bar, enter "file:/" followed by the location of your document. You can then save this location in your bookmarks, so you don't have to type the entire address again. When calling up files, capitalization must be exact.

When you're not online or have no wireless service and you need to access your files, proceed as if you'd like to connect, then simply press the circle button to kill the Internet Browser page load. Then press the triangle button to bring up the menu and follow the same directions as described above.

You have two means of saving files onto your Memory Stick: **save link target** and **save image**. Position your cursor over the page link or image you want to save, press the triangle button and then bring up the **File** menu. By default, link targets will save to your Common folder, while images will save to your Photo folder. But you can both rename your file and choose its destination – be especially careful where you save the files. For instance, video files aren't placed in the seemingly obvious Video folder, and are instead housed in a subfolder of the frighteningly named MP_ROOT directory (see p.71).

Bookmarks: Your thumbs' best friends

Bookmarks

The Internet Browser lets you save and edit your bookmarks, and with the right program you can import bookmarks from your computer's browser – a real time saver considering the limitations of the typepad interface. You can also export your bookmarks directly from your computer's browser by hand – both Internet Explorer and Safari can do this quite easily. Choose **Export Bookmarks** from the File menu on your browser, name the resulting file "bookmarks.html," and replace any similarly named file in your PSP's Browser folder. Note that doing this will overwrite any bookmarks you already saved using the PSP's browser.

> **TIP** If the browser hangs while downloading a site, press the Home button and you'll be taken back to the PSP's main menu.

View: Changing the way your screen looks

More and more websites are designing their pages to fit the PSP screen. But the majority of places you'll go haven't taken such steps. There are a few ways you can reduce page clutter and cut down on disorienting four-way scrolling.

Using the **Display Mode** feature, you can adjust the page contents to Just-Fit – where the browser squeezes all horizontal content onto the PSP screen; or Smart-Fit – where all the content is stacked on top of each other in something approximating its original girth. You can also adjust text size (or select your primary language) in the Encoding option.

Just-Fit

Normal-Fit

Alternatively, stick to sites with page content optimized for the PSP's screen. Beyond the obvious example of the official PSP site, there are a number of other Web pages dedicated to distributing Web content in PSP screen format – see below. You can find more on this topic in the Extending section, including how to create your own PSP-ready Web pages (see p.134).

Sony PlayStation www.playstation.com
Web to PSP www.webtopsp.com
PSP Web Browser www.pspwebbrowser.com
PSP Connect http://psp.connect.com
Hacking the PSP http://hackingpsp.com
PSPset www.pspset.com
WorldView www.longfingers.com/psp
PSP Drive www.pspdrive.com/psp

Tools: This is where I set my homepage?

Under the Tools menu you'll find a **Settings** option, where you're given control over your cookies, the cache size, your history status, and, most importantly, your homepage. For the most part, you won't have cause to fiddle with many of these save the homepage, with the occasional history purge to clean up after yourself.

From time to time you may get an "out of memory" warning when you're trying to load a page. If you don't mind pictureless websites, you can relieve some memory strain by turning off images and animations in the **View Settings** option. You can also set the cache at a low level to increase the available memory, but doing so will slow down reloads of previously visited sites.

One final Settings tool – you can set a specific proxy server for use with your browser, regardless of the one chosen in your network settings (see p.93). Proxy servers assign you a fake IP address, making it almost impossible to identify where your PSP is physically located – very helpful if you're concerned about people tracking your Web movements and discovering your secret lair.

RSS

 If you want to listen to a BBC 5 audio feed through the Internet Browser, you're out of luck. It's simply not powerful enough to work with helper applications like RealAudio and QuickTime that handle the media content on your computer's Web browser. There are more advanced ways of streaming audio to your computer over the Internet (see p.136), but PSPs with firmware versions 2.60 and higher come with a handy RSS (Really Simple Syndication) feature, making it easy to listen to streaming **podcasts**.

When you come across an audio feed with an **XML**, **Atom**, or **RSS** icon next to it, just click on the icon and the Internet Browser will save its location in your RSS channel list. While still connected to the Internet, head to the PSP's RSS function, click your saved channel, and within seconds the stream flows forth. Should you jump ahead and try to run the RSS feature without first saving any feeds, you'll be taken through a brief tutorial explaining just how simple it all really is.

Here are some RSS directories and some specific streaming audio feeds to check out:

XML ATOM

NETWORKING

PSP Podcast www.podpsp.com
Penguin Radio www.penguinradio.com/rss
SubPop www.subpop.com/multimedia/freeradiosp.php
NPR www.npr.org/rss/podcast/podcast_directory.php
BBC radio www.bbc.co.uk/radio/
Virgin Radio www.virginradioxtreme.co.uk/thestation/podcast
The Onion www.theonion.com/content/feeds/radionews

RSS 2.0 It's even possible to set up your own computer as a server and stream your music to the PSP (see p.136).

TIP Versions of firmware 2.7 and above give the option of downloading and saving podcasts. Rather than having to listen to them as they stream, you can listen to saved podcasts anywhere, anytime, without having to be connected to the Internet.

FIRMWARE,
SOFTWARE
& HOMEBREW

△
□
○
✕

14

Firmware

operating systems matter

Firmware is another name for the system software, essentially the operating system of your PSP. It's the firmware that tells your PSP how to load UMDs, access the Memory Stick, display photos, and the like. The PSP's menu system is the graphical user interface (GUI) of the firmware: just like Windows XP or Mac OSX on your computer, what you see is not the operating system itself, but a visual representation that allows the device to be used intuitively. You may not think there's much more to be said, but Sony has produced eight different versions of firmware for the English-speaking market since the PSP debuted in 2004, and which version you run affects, and in many ways defines, what you can do with your PSP. As well as offering different features and supporting different media formats, your firmware version also determines how and whether you will be able to run homebrew programs – emulators and other independently written programs for the PSP.

A BRIEF HISTORY OF FIRMWARE

The first PSPs released in Japan towards the end of 2004 ran firmware version 1.00, naturally enough. However, when the PSP reached other markets, including the US and the UK, it was with version 1.50 installed. To Sony's dismay, an oversight allowed version 1.00 devices (which are virtually nonexistent these days) to run what's known as "unsigned code," which means that programmers didn't need to use Sony's development kit or encryption key to write software for the PSP. Version 1.50 isn't quite such an easy proposition for programmers, but is susceptible to a minor exploit that's included in all homebrew software. These two early versions are unique among PSP firmware in allowing the user to easily run homebrew software – unofficial software for the PSP written by independent programmers that includes everything from emulators for the NES to PSP drum machines.

Sony, however, is not a fan of "unauthorized software," and patched the hole that let users run homebrew with versions 1.51 and 1.52, which came installed on all new PSPs. Significant new features, such as a web browser and support for a wider array of media formats, came with version 2.00, providing the first real incentive to upgrade from older versions. Sony didn't quite close all the doors, though, since it's possible to revert from 2.00 back to 1.50. This was rectified with version 2.01: from 2.01 onwards, there's no going back.

Starting in the fall of 2005, Sony began to include firmware updates with new games, such as Grand Theft Auto: Liberty City Stories, requiring you to update your PSP in order to play them. This, along with the new features included in each firmware update, has led many more users to run the most recent version of firmware.

The newest version of firmware when this book went to print was 2.70, which includes everything from an Internet browser to the ability to download podcasts, to watching streaming digital video. It's a big step up from 1.50 in terms of capability, but as you'll see, there can be compelling reasons to run older firmware as well.

> **TIP** Aside from region encoding for movies (see p.27), there is no other apparent difference in firmware from different parts of the world. 2.70 is 2.70 everywhere you go.

WHICH VERSION TO CHOOSE?

If you're buying a new PSP, you don't have much of a choice – all new PSPs ship with version 2.01 or later. To find out which firmware version yours is running, go to the **Settings** menu of the PSP. Navigate to **System Settings**, select **System Information**, and you'll see a screen that identifies the MAC Address of your PSP (its unique network identifier), the System Software (which will be listed as anything from 1.50 to 2.70), and your PSP's Nickname (which you gave it when you set it up).

Any decision to change your firmware should be based on the features you want your PSP to have. There are three firmware versions you can simply discount: versions 1.51, 1.52, and 2.01 don't offer any new features and preclude you from using old features (or exploits, as the case may be). Otherwise, the choice is between upgrading to the latest version or opting for 1.50. There are only two ways to do the latter: buy an old PSP online (see p.12 for advice), or, if you have 2.00, 1.51, or 1.52, it's possible to downgrade to 1.50 (see p.115).

The downside to 1.50 is that you can't play most recent UMD games, nor can you use the PSP's emerging capabilities, for instance downloading podcasts or viewing streaming video. If, on

FIRMWARE, SOFTWARE & HOMEBREW

the other hand, you want to play ROMs (copies of video games for old systems like the NES), use your PSP as a remote control for your TV or other devices, or are intending to write software yourself, you'll want to go for version 1.50. Most homebrew development is for version 1.50, since this version lets you easily run software. See the chart below for details on the features (and restrictions) that each version of firmware offers.

FIRMWARE CHART

	Video	Music	Photos
1.50	MP4	MP3	JPEG
1.51	MP4	MP3	JPEG
1.52	MP4	MP3	JPEG
2.00	MP4, AVC	MP3, ATRAC3plus, AAC, WAV	JPEG, TIFF, GIF, PNG, BMP image transfer, wallpaper
2.01	MP4, AVC	MP3, ATRAC3plus, AAC, WAV	JPEG, TIFF, GIF, PNG, BMP image transfer, wallpaper
2.50	MP4, AVC	MP3, ATRAC3plus, AAC, WAV	JPEG, TIFF, GIF, PNG, BMP image transfer, wallpaper
2.60	MP4, AVC	MP3, ATRAC3plus, AAC, WAV, WMA	JPEG, TIFF, GIF, PNG, BMP image transfer, wallpaper
2.70	MP4, AVC	MP3, ATRAC3plus, AAC, WAV, WMA	JPEG, TIFF, GIF, PNG, BMP image transfer, wallpaper

We've not included games in this chart, as it's impossible to attach them to a version of firmware with any certainty. For more info on playing new games on old firmware, see p.59.

THE TWO-PSP SOLUTION

As crazy as it sounds, there's a growing number of people who own two PSPs. The reason is simple – they don't want to make the hard choices about upgrading their firmware, and they have enough money to buy a second one. If you do have the cash, it's not a bad solution. You can keep one PSP at 1.50 in order to run homebrew and explore homebrew development. The other you can continue to upgrade with the latest version to take advantage of new capabilities and play new games as they come along.

RSS (podcasts)	Web browser	Homebrew	Downgradable
No	No	Yes	No
No	No	No	Yes [2]
No	No	Yes	Yes [2]
No	Yes	Yes [1]	Yes
No	Yes	Yes [1]	No
No	Yes	Yes [1]	No
Yes, streaming	Yes	Yes [1]	No
Yes, downloadable	Yes	No (at press time)	No

[1] most emulators, some games and applications, no UMD loaders
[2] only after upgrading to 2.0

UPGRADING FIRMWARE

Sony has sort of closed up the PSP. There are no clear mechanisms by which you can change your firmware, run other operating systems, and so forth – but you can always get the newest firmware through official Sony updates. Whether you should however, is for you to decide. Here are the various ways you can do it.

Using a UMD

One of the easiest ways to update your firmware is to use the firmware updates that come on certain UMD games. For example: when we got GTA: Liberty City Stories and wanted to play it on our Version 1.50 PSP, we used the 2.00 firmware upgrade that came on the UMD. Newer games come with newer versions of the firmware – make sure you think about which version you want before upgrading, since if you go above 2.00, you won't be able to change back again.

> **TIP** When upgrading your firmware, always make sure your PSP is fully charged, and plugged in using the AC adaptor.

To perform the update from the UMD, go to the **Game** menu, navigate to the icon labeled "**PSP Update ver X.XX**," select it, and follow the instructions. The update will work its magic, and within a few minutes you'll be running the new firmware.

Using Network Update

The Network Update option, accessed from the **Settings** menu, uses your WiFi connection to download an update of the firmware from Sony. Only the most recent version is available this way and, if you haven't done this already, you'll need to create network settings (see p.93). Sony provides a clear tutorial on upgrading this way on its PSP website: **www.playstation.com**.

Official downloads

You can download the most recent firmware update to your computer from the Sony PSP website. You can find full instructions there, but all you need to do is create a folder called **Update** inside your **Game** folder on the Memory Stick. Download the firmware and copy it to that **Game ▶ Update** folder. Take your PSP out of USB mode, go to the **Game** menu, select the firmware update, launch it, and in short order the new firmware will be on your PSP.

Unofficial downloads

While Sony always offers the most recent update, thanks to the magic of the Internet, nothing is ever lost; you can find every version of the firmware available for download from unofficial outlets. You may consider this option if, for example, you want to upgrade from 1.50 to 2.00 in order to play certain games. As with most unofficial processes, this will void your PSP's warranty. And messing around with your firmware is one of the more dangerous things you can do – it's very possible to brick your PSP. But if you're willing to accept the risk, you can poke around and find a number of options. Some websites that have a good reputation for firmware downloads include:

QJ.net http://dl.qj.net/PSP-Firmwares/catid/163
psp-hacks.com www.psp-hacks.com/category/10

DOWNGRADING FIRMWARE

While upgrading is easy, downgrading is less so. You can downgrade only version 2.00 of the firmware, and you have to do it through a somewhat scary procedure that, at first glance, appears to wreck your PSP. Downgrading firmware is strongly discouraged by Sony, too, so why bother? Because it's the only way to revert some PSPs (namely those running 1.51, 1.52, and 2.0) to 1.50, the firmware version that runs most homebrew smoothly and easily – if this is what you want to do. However scary it looks, it can be done safely, and once you know how, you can actually switch firmware back and forth between 2.00 and 1.50 with relative ease.

Don't underestimate the risks involved, though. If something goes awry with your firmware downgrade (or upgrade, for that matter), your PSP won't work anymore and no commonly available method exists for repairing the device at this point. If something goes wrong when upgrading with official updates, Sony will probably fix your PSP for free if it's under warranty. If something goes wrong when downgrading, Sony might repair it, but it'll cost you. It's your PSP, though, and as long as you're willing to assume the risks, you can give it a shot.

> **TIP** Don't try downgrading your firmware if you're running 2.01 or later. It's not going to work, at least not with any of the methods available at press time, and will likely destroy your PSP. That said, PSP hackers are relentlessly pursuing this goal and a search online for "downgrading PSP firmware" will turn up the status of any current ongoing work.

To perform the downgrade, you need to get hold of two things: a program called MPH Downgrader, available from QJ.net, or direct from the programmer at **http://mphwebsite.tuxfamily.org**; and the 1.50 firmware update, also available from QJ.net or from **psp-hacks.com**.

How to do it

In order to downgrade to version 1.50, you must be running 1.51, 1.52, or 2.00. Check your firmware before beginning. If you're at 2.00, you're ready to start. If you're running 1.51 or 1.52, you must first find a 2.00 firmware update and upgrade your PSP (see p.115). You cannot downgrade directly from 1.51 or 1.52.

BRICK ALERT!

While we're unaware of much virus development for the PSP, there is one Trojan program that is possible to launch inadvertently when downgrading. It gets onto your PSP the same way that the MPH Downgrader does, but instead of hooking you up with a way to get 1.50 firmware, it deletes files and renders your PSP useless. Avoid anything that is authored by a group called "PSP Team."

For greatest reliability, download the MPH Downgrader directly from their website. Be warned that Symantec security software identifies the MPH program as a virus, since it uses the same exploit. You may have to disable your security software in order to get the downgrade files for your PSP. Symantec has information about the Trojan here: www.sarc.com/avcenter/venc/data/trojan.pspbrick.html

Additionally, in early 2005 there was a firmware update floating around, authored by Sony but still in developmental stages. If you come across an unofficial update that promises you a word processor or mail program, stay away. And if the unofficial update that you've started to install says that it's going to add these features, stop right there. Your PSP is still safe at that point, so quit the process, delete the files, and don't use them again.

Note that while these are the only things we've come across that can significantly damage your PSP through its firmware, that doesn't mean there aren't others either already out there or in development. It's worth spending some time doing research on PSP bulletin boards to check whether any other viruses or Trojans have been released.

• First, download the MPH Downgrader and the 1.50 EBOOT file, which you will use later to restore 1.50 firmware to your PSP.

• Create an **Update** folder in your **Game** folder, and put the 1.50 EBOOT file there.

• Unzip the MPH Downgrader package, and copy the "overflow.tif" file into your **Photo** folder.

• Copy the "h.bin" and "index.dat" files onto the root of your Memory Stick (the main folder you get when you open the Memory Stick on your computer).

• Ready? Exit USB mode and plug in your AC Adaptor.

• Navigate to your Photo menu on the PSP and select Memory Stick. What you see will look like your PSP has had some weird crash – your screen goes black and will display three rows of characters on the left side of your screen. Scary, sure, but your PSP is probably still ok.

• Wait for at least 30 seconds and restart your PSP. Hold your power switch up for about ten seconds to force the PSP to power down. Give it a moment, and turn it back on.

• Plug your PSP back into your computer. Enter **USB Mode**, and check that you have a file called "index.dat.bak" in your Memory Stick's root. If so, continue.

• Navigate to the **Game** menu, and select **Memory Stick**. You should see an option to update using **PSP Update ver. 1.50**. It will tell you what features come with 1.50.

• Press the right button on the D-pad to get to the next screen. It'll give you a warning about not interrupting the process. Make sure your AC adaptor is plugged in, and press the X button to continue.

• Your PSP will now update as if it was doing so for any other version of firmware. But when it's about to finish – at about 99% complete – your PSP will appear to crash. Your screen will say "The update failed." Do not panic, this is normal.

• Restart your PSP by turning it off or forcing it to power down, and turning it back on. You'll see a screen with the same message in a number of languages – it will tell you that "Setting information is corrupted." Ignore this message.

• It will also tell you to press the circle button to "repair and restore default settings." Press circle. It should take about a minute or so to reboot. If it doesn't, manually restart the PSP by forcing it to power down again. Turn it back on, and repeat.

• Proceed with setting up your PSP, and you should be good to go!

ONLINE TUTORIALS

With the knowledge you might render your beloved PSP useless, down-grading the firmware is inevitably a daunting prospect. Whereas MPH Downgrader comes with clear instructions as to where you should put the various files, they don't really explain what comes next. If you'd like the reas-surance of seeing what the screen is supposed to look like when you get the ominous messages that "The update failed" and "Setting information is corrupted," check out the following websites:

afterdawn.com www.afterdawn.com/guides/archive/downgrade_psp_2.cfm
QJ.net http://forums.qj.net
MPH http://mphwebsite.tuxfamily.org

15

Software

maximize your PSP

The PSP is a pretty powerful system given its extreme portability. Its processor speed can reach 333 MegaHertz, and while it has virtually no internal storage, the advent of 4GB and 8GB Memory Sticks means that you can carry around a fair amount of data and run some comparatively large programs.

WHAT SOFTWARE IS AVAILABLE?

Since Sony, naturally, feels that it should be the pre-eminent developer of software for the system, there are few PSP programs available from the big-name software companies. Media players like iTunes and RealPlayer can't be used on the PSP; nor are there word processing programs like Microsoft Word or WordPerfect for the device. Video game developers, on the other hand, are producing UMD games for the PSP at a fairly rapid clip – see p.40.

There are, however, some very useful – and interesting – programs available for the PSP. The major streams of development have been in media managers that run on your computer and in homebrew. The former help you organize, prepare, and transfer your digital media files. The latter, which includes emulators for legacy video games systems (see p.48 for an in-depth discussion of these), is the term for programs written by independent programmers, hackers, and a handful of third-party developers, that run right on your PSP.

MEDIA MANAGERS

The PSP may allow you to watch feature-length films, play songs, and view and share photos from the Memory Stick, but getting this array of content on there, in the correct format, isn't always easy. For example, handling photos is relatively simple and intuitive, while dealing with video files can be a real pain. We cover video, audio, and photo content in much greater detail in their respective chapters, including some free ways to convert video and DVD files for your PSP. For around twenty dollars, though, a media manager can take a lot of the hassle and frustration out of the process, making it a worthwhile investment, especially if you want to play around with or use a lot of video content on your PSP. Sony produces its own media manager, but it doesn't come bundled with the PSP.

> **TIP** Media managers don't always allow you to convert DVDs directly into PSP-viewable files. As a Mac user, you'll need a program like Handbrake, and for Windows, a program like PSP Movie Creator will do the trick. See p.68 for more on DVD conversion.

Sony PSP Media Manager
Sony's offering in the field of media management is solid, with features that are common to most of the programs, including photo conversion (though this isn't really necessary unless you're run-

ning version 1.50 of the firmware). It easily converts a wide variety of video formats into MP4 or AVC files that are viewable on your PSP, and as with all media managers, backs up your game saves.

The program has two particularly useful features. First, there's a built-in CD extraction feature, so if you don't already have a CD on your computer as MP3 files, the PSP Media Manager will convert them for you and get the album, artist, and track information using Gracenote (the same online database iTunes uses to get its information). Second, you can subscribe to audio and video podcasts and have them prepared for one-click transfer to your PSP. No need to download, convert, and transfer them through the usual route – PSP Media Manager handles the whole thing for you.

Sony PSP Media Manager www.sonymediasoftware.com/Products $19.95. Windows only

PSPWare

PSPWare is an efficient media manager for both Mac and Windows users. Unlike the Sony offering, it syncs with iTunes, allowing all of your unprotected music to be moved to your PSP. It also syncs with both iPhoto and Windows Picture folders, making transferring photos even easier. Most common video formats are supported for conversion into a PSP-viewable format via drag-and-drop. And of course, it offers the standard game backup feature.

More unusually, the program will sync bookmarks from Safari, Firefox, Internet Explorer, and more to your PSP, so you can avoid the tedium of having to manually enter each address. You can also create different "Sync profiles" for different Memory Sticks, so the program won't automatically update a Memory Stick with content that you've set up for a different one.

PSPWare www.nullriver.com/index/products/pspware
Feature-limited trial version free; full version $15.
Windows and Mac

iPSP

A company called RnSKSoftronics makes iPSP, an extremely intuitive program with an interface Mac users will find particularly familiar. For both Windows and Mac, it supports drag-and-drop file transfer and conversion for a variety of audio and photo formats, and you can set up your video preferences such that your video files convert at the quality and in the format you prefer.

Unlike the other media managers, iPSP supports conversion from VIDEO_TS and DVD Video Object (.vob) files – the type of video files found on DVDs. This can make it much easier to convert your DVDs into PSP-ready files; for more on this, see p.68.

IPSP http://ipsp.kaisakura.com/ipsp.php
Feature-limited trial version free; full version $19.99.
Windows and Mac

16

Homebrew

fill up on freeware

Homebrew, as with the individually made ales and stouts that are its namesake, varies widely in quality – all that ties it together is that it's software that's been written specifically to run on the PSP. It allows you to do dozens of things with the device, from playing old video games to listening to Internet radio stations.

WHAT IS HOMEBREW?

When the PSP was first released, computer programmers worldwide investigated its potential uses, quickly discovering that the first version of the firmware (1.00) allowed the PSP to run unsigned code, and the second (1.50) had an easy workaround that's almost invisible to users. Able to develop software without Sony's approval or authorization, the homebrew community was born, and today numbers a fairly large group of people writing programs specifically for the PSP.

For the most part, homebrew is written for version 1.50 of the PSP's firmware, which is why you often come across PSPs in the used market advertised as having that firmware – and why they're often sold at a premium. How many PSPs are running version 1.50 is hard to say, but it's a limited number, and the people who own them really do like being able to play emulators and run quirky little programs for the device. See p.110 for a history of firmware, and p.112 for a chart showing which versions support homebrew and to what extent.

The homebrew community is, like most communities of hackers, at once competitive and collaborative. People share information, and build upon it, but at the same time try to be the first to develop new types of homebrew or new ways to access it. It's vibrant and extremely fast-moving: as we worked on this book, we followed the development of numerous homebrew applications – Fanjita getting eLoader to work on the 2.60 firmware upgrade (see p.128) and the development of ways to play games that require 2.60 firmware on 1.50 machines, among many, many more. Check the various homebrew and PSP websites regularly for the most up-to-date information about homebrew apps, games, and ongoing development. Homebrew developers are often first to come up with new features for the PSP, before these are included in a firmware update.

The relationship between the homebrew community and Sony is strained at best. But aside from voiding the warranty of PSPs that run homebrew and requiring PSP users to upgrade their firmware to play the latest games, Sony hasn't yet taken extensive or legal action against homebrew developers and users.

125

TIP If you're a programmer interested in this kind of development, the PS2DEV forums are a great resource: **http://forums.ps2dev.org**. Also check out Scriptscribbler, which offers a thorough tutorial introducing programming for the PSP: **http://www.scriptscribbler.com/psp**.

WHAT KIND OF HOMEBREW IS OUT THERE?

Homebrew breaks down, essentially, into the categories of games and applications. Some games, like Doom, have been ported to the PSP; others are playable through emulators, technically applications that allow you to play games that you find on ROM files, although for the purposes of this book, we've grouped them with games. See p.59 for an in-depth discussion of homebrew emulators.

Homebrew applications come in a huge variety of forms. There are audiovisual applications like PSPRadio, which lets you listen to some Internet radio stations using your PSP (see p.136), and PSPRhythm, which turns your PSP into a drum machine (see p.134); programs like File Assistant, which lets you manage your Memory Stick content directly from your PSP, making it possible to move files without using your computer; PSP Universal Remote, which can let you control your TV and cable box using the PSP's IR port (see p.139); and there's even an Instant Messaging client for the PSP – it's called PSPChat, and you can use it to IM with other PSPChat users.

WHERE CAN IT BE DOWNLOADED?

Homebrew programs and games can be found all over the Internet. Because homebrew developers generally want to encourage both use of their programs and development of the homebrew community in general, they tend to provide clear instructions for installation and use (as a .txt text file) along with the downloaded program.

The sites listed below are some of the best for homebrew to download. Note also that sites using the torrent method of distribution (see **www.bittorrent.com** for more about torrents) also have homebrew in abundance. In order to use these, you need a BitTorrent client, like BitTorrent itself, Azureus, or any of the numerous other clients online, some of which claim to be faster than others.

FREEWARE ETIQUETTE

Homebrew software is what's known as freeware or shareware. The programs are free – you needn't pay anybody to download them, and there are no restrictions on their use. In fact, code is often left open via GNU licenses – an agreement among freeware developers that attempts to ensure that the freeware remains free, and also encourages other developers to build upon their work.

However, you'll often come across websites or homebrew documentation that requests a donation. While freeware is, well, free, homebrew developers have put a lot of time, effort, and sometimes money into developing their programs. Making a donation is a good way to thank them for their efforts and to support future homebrew development. Same holds for the developers of other freeware we recommend in this book, such as Handbrake or ffmpegX.

Download sites

PSP-hacks www.psp-hacks.com
PSP Brew www.pspbrew.com
PSPHacks www.psphacks.net
The Pirate Bay http://thepiratebay.org
TorrentBox www.torrentbox.com

Online homebrew help

PSP-hacks www.psp-hacks.com/sony-psp-homebrew-tutorial.php
Scriptscribbler www.scriptscribbler.com/psp/guide/installing-homebrew.htm

Minimizing the risks

As always, you should consider the risks involved with downloading and running software on your computer or PSP. Computers, particularly Windows PCs, are highly susceptible to malware – viruses, worms, etc, that are designed to harm your computer. There doesn't seem to be much malware written for the PSP itself, aside from the Trojan downgrader (see p.117).

When you're poking around for homebrew, pay attention. Read comments about a program you're considering on the forum of the download website. Research the program and, if possible, the programmer (if they don't have a real name, you can usually find their handle). See whether other users have had luck with it, and make sure nobody has reported that their PSP has been "bricked" by using the program. Doing some homework could well save you from a disaster that means you have to replace your PSP.

FANJITA & DITLEW

A programmer going by the handle Fanjita is world-renowned for creating eLoader (see p.56 in the Games section), a program that enables people using firmware versions other than 1.50 to run homebrew games and applications on their PSPs. Ditlew has also worked on the program, most recently on improving the eLoader menu interface. Their renown is due to the fact that eLoader has effectively kept homebrew alive for people who otherwise wouldn't have been able to use it.

eLoader, intentionally, does not support UMD rippers or loaders; since it therefore can't be used to actively pirate PSP games, the program seems to be on solid legal footing. For information about eLoader, including a discussion forum and a list of which homebrew programs are compatible, visit their website.

Fanjita & Ditlew, aka "Noobz" http://noobz.eu

EXTRAS

△
□
○
✕

17

Extending the PSP

a little something more

In earlier chapters on media content and the Internet, we discussed a number of ways to do more with your PSP than Sony originally intended. In this chapter, you'll find even more unique software and hardware modifications that will further extend the PSP's capabilities. And while we've made every attempt at including the most current versions of everything we list, new developments happen all the time, and programs, specifically, are continually improved and quickly distributed – aided in no small part by the strong sharing principles of the PSP homebrew community. If you go looking for any of the items we mention only to find that a newer version is available, make sure it will work with your firmware, and refer to the Resources section for additional help (see p.193).

EXTEND... THE INTERNET

Instant Messaging

The PSP's Internet Browser was not even a year old when this book was written, and for such a new feature it performs very well. But, as we discussed earlier, the PSP is currently incapable of playing Internet audio or video in the same way your computer's Web browser can (see p.105). It's also unable to support Instant Messenger programs, which

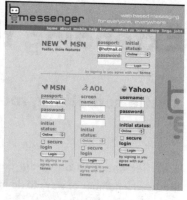

would be useful in such a portable device, even though the type-pad is not exactly fun to use. While you can't download AIM or YahooIM onto your PSP, you can use it to navigate to some Web pages that will help you log onto your Instant Messenger account, view your list of online friends, and send and receive notes.

eMessenger www.e-messenger.net
AIMOnPSP www.penguinprofile.com/aim

There was as recently as April 2006 an **IRC** (Internet Relay Channel) portal at **PSP IRC** (www.pspirc.com) maintained by Robert Balousek, but while we were writing this book he was forced to take it down due to abuses to the system. Balousek fully intends to resurrect his IRC portal, and has been actively seeking server space, so it's worth checking from time to time to see if it's back up.

Graphic novels online

There are a number of websites designed to fit the PSP's screen perfectly (see p.104), and some of the most popular have broken new ground by merging old and new media formats. For instance, many comics and graphic novels have gone online, including a massive amount of scanned and translated **manga**. And while major comics publishers offer both printed and Web-based stories, they've been slow to format their online offerings for the PSP. On the other hand, some smaller creators have begun to release their content exclusively through much less expensive Internet channels, with pages designed specifically for the PSP's screen.

Web sites with libraries of scanned manga and comic books may not have the right to distribute said content, so if you want to at least partially absolve yourself of copyright infringement, you shouldn't download the files – just read them online. When you do find legal content available for download, you'll need to make sure all the files can be understood by the PSP (see p.85), and that you save them into the right place on your Memory Stick (see p.33). And while you can download and save files directly from the Web with your PSP (see p.101), a quicker, more reliable method is to use your computer for the download, and then transfer the files over to your PSP using process described in the Photos chapter (see p.87).

NYC 2123 was the first graphic novel created for the PSP.

NYC 2123 www.nyc2123.com
ARComics http://arcomics.com
Geneon Animation www.geneonanimation.com/psp
Manga Downloads www.mangadownloads.org
Mangascreener www.mangascreener.com
Komikerks www.komikwerks.com
Online Comics www.onlinecomics.net

If you have your own website and want to make it PSP-friendly, you can find the browser specifications (such as HTML version support, JavaScript limitations, and image sizing guidelines) on the Sony Europe support site **www.technology.scee.net/psp_browser_ guidelines.**

EXTRAS

> **TIP** If you come across a great read that isn't quite screen friendly, you can use the **Just-Fit** or **Smart-Fit** option to make the content better conform to your PSP's screen (see p.104).

EXTEND...THE AUDIO

Creating rhythms

If you have aspirations to recording or DJ fame, you'll be happy to know you have a new sound generator to add to the mix. You can make your own beats with the Iturzaeta brothers' **PSP Rhythm** (www.psprhythm.com), a 16 step drum machine with a bass synthesizer modeled after the iconic Roland 303 – the machine responsible for the acid house sound from the 1980s. This extremely clever homebrew application allows remarkable control over beat patterns and sound effects, supports measure by measure editing, and records your finished songs in a format easily handled by Windows and Mac computers.

PSP Rhythm comes with a number of pre-installed drum kits, but you can also create your own kits using any sound samples. A full discussion of sampling and recording music is outside the scope of this book, but a Google search for "home recording" will yield a plethora of helpful resources. You can also find a good discussion of drum machines and beat-making, and helpful advice on all aspects of the program itself in the PSP Rhythm forums (**www.psprhythm.com/forum**).

EXTRAS

135

INSTALLING PSP RHYTHM

As is the case for a lot of well-developed homebrew applications, PSP Rhythm has an automatic PSP installer option for Windows users, while Mac users will have to perform a manual install. Unfortunately, the manual install instructions on the site are no help for anyone using eLoader (see p.56). But thanks to a fellow named Rykor, we're able to give you a nice easy set of instructions that work like a charm. (These instructions assume you already have eLoader .97 installed on your PSP, and that you have downloaded the PSP Rhythm 5 files from **www.psprhythm.com**.)

1. Connect your PSP to your computer (see p.7).
2. Click on the PSP Rhythm 5 folder that you downloaded; inside you'll see three subfolders: "1.0 and 2.0+," "1.5," and "rhythm."
3. Copy the "rhythm" folder to your PSP's Game folder.
4. Inside the "1.0 and 2.0+" folder you'll find a file called "eboot.pbp" – copy that into the "rhythm" folder you just placed in your PSP's Game folder.
5. Run eLoader, select PSP Rhythm, start jamming.

MON PETIT CHOU

Talkman, a USB accessory produced by Sony ($60/£35) that comes with a UMD language-learning game and translation tool, was inspired by its creator's inability to successfully pull foreign women. Using its microphone and a program that can understand the spoken word, Talkman's Japanese release can help translate your pick-up lines from English into Japanese, Korean, or Chinese, while the European version covers Italian, Spanish, German, French, and Japanese. And its learning mode quizzes you on the pronunciation of a variety of common phrases and words, grading your ability to speak them clearly and coherently.

Streaming audio

There are many different types of audio files swimming through the Internet – and just as many programs used to catch them. We've discussed the capabilities of the PSP's RSS function (see p.105), but if you're running firmware version 1.50 you have another option – Raf's **PSPRadio**. With this homebrew application connected to the Internet you can listen to thousands of streaming SHOUTcast radio stations, covering every imaginable genre of music (as long as your Internet connection is steady, that is). If you want to broadcast your own radio program over the Internet, the SHOUTcast website has instructions on how to set up your computer to stream music.

Chances are you have an iPod, and you probably use iTunes to organize and synchronize your music. Wouldn't it be nice to sync your PSP with iTunes as well? Enter **DOT-Tunes**, a program that helps you set up your computer as a server, and creates a webpage that lists your iTunes catalog by artist or album. Then, using the PSP's Internet Browser, you can download your well organized iTunes library into the Music folder on your PSP's Memory Stick (see p.75).

PSPRadio http://rafpsp.blogspot.com
Shoutcast www.shoutcast.com
DOT-Tunes www.dotpod.net
DCLVXI Productions www.dclxvi.nl/psp_rss

EXTEND... THE VIDEO

TV adaptors

137

We've explained how to transfer videos between your computer and the PSP (see p.66), but what if, instead of watching videos on the PSP, you want to display the PSP's screen on a television so everyone can see? Or maybe you want to capture a still from a UMD video without having to isolate yourself in a darkened room with a super-megapixel camera? There are a couple of ways to achieve these feats: you can either attach a television/video converter directly to the PSP's internal circuitry; or you can buy an attachment that fits over the screen and doesn't void your warranty.

The easy way is to buy a screw-on, hooded attachment that fits over the face of the PSP and records its screen with a video camera. There are three on the market: The Blaze TV adaptor, PSPonTV, and the Nyko Play on TV, all roughly the same price ($50/£30), and each with similar sets of composite video and stereo ports. This method's only downside, albeit a minor one, is that you don't gain an additional monitor (like with the Xtender model, see overleaf), since you'll have hidden the PSP screen under a hood while transferring the video output to a larger display.

DIY TV ADAPTOR

Feeling handy? You can make your own hood and mount a video camera inside set to match the PSP screen's 30 frames per second (fps) refresh rate. Even older video cameras will have all the cable connections you'll need to attach to a television – if you have an old one lying around that you don't use, it may not be such a bad little project to try. If successful, send your achievement to one of the gadget blogs we mention in Resources (see p.176), and you're likely to receive a brief splash of Internet fame.

If you reject the easy option, intent instead on digging into places maybe you shouldn't (see p.148), you'll be either happy or slightly disappointed to know that a readymade video converter is available for connecting to your PSP's internal circuitry. Team Xtender's PSP2TV sells for $120, and the installation process will void your warranty, but it does offer both composite and S-video ports, as well as stereo outs, and it even accepts a PS2 controller. The bulk of the adaptor sits center-back, and doesn't affect the balance by much, and images show on the PSP and TV at same time, so you can look at either display.

Blaze TV adaptor www.xploder.net/psp
PSPonTV www.pspontv.com
Nyko Play on TV www.nyko.com/nyko/products
PSP2TV www.teamxtender.com

Screen captures

Just reached the highest of the high scores and don't have a video converter? Take a screen capture during game play with Nekokabu's PSP screen capture program (**http://nekokabu.s7.xrea. com**) and email the results to your friends. For now this program only works on version 1.50 firmware, but new homebrew developments happen all the time.

EXTEND... **THE IR PORT**

The IR (Infra Red) port has no official uses, but then again the PSP's hardware is only as capable as its software allows. There are plenty of unofficial homebrew uses for the IR port, all perfectly fine to operate within the bounds of law. Of course, getting the IR port to do something useful can be an easy or extremely complicated affair depending on exactly what your intentions are.

Remote controller

The simplest way to get some use out of your IR port is to find a pre-packaged PSP remote control homebrew program, like **PSP Remote**. If you have a second generation PS2 (the ones with the built-in IR port), a quick download and install of PSP Remote will let you to control the PS2's games and DVDs with your PSP. The program also gives you command over Sony WEGA televisions, bringing the WEGA remote menu up on your PSP's screen. And since everything is already packaged, you don't need to bother with any special "coding" at all. To find this little gem, head to **QJ.Net** (**http://dl.qj. net**) and do a search for "PSP remote control." QJ.net also houses the files for the **PSP Universal Remote** – another plug-and-play remote option containing commands for a wide array of video and audio components – a similar search will yield its location.

A more inventive way to go about IR blasting is with **iR Shell**, a program that simply opens the IR port for your use, leaving you to run remote control packages downloaded from elsewhere, like the **Xbox 360 controller**. Alternatively, you can write your own code for iR Shell so that your PSP can operate your audio and video components at home. This option shouldn't be entered into lightly as it's not as simple as loading a program into the proper folder on your Memory Stick. You'll have to cut and paste strings of Pronto Hex keys – numbers that represent remote control functions like volume up and power off. If you do want to try this, you'll find instructions in the iR Shell's readme documentation, plus loads of keys for current devices at Remote Central.

QJ.Net http://dl.qj.ne
iR Shell www.ahman.co.nr
Remote Central www.sunstorm.com/remote
Xbox 360 controller http://forums.qj.net/showthread.php?t=45644

TIP iR Shell also lets two PSPs exchange files through their IR ports. It's a very slow process, though, and it makes much more sense to swap files across a computer if one is available.

EXTEND... THE OPERATING SYSTEM

The PSP is a powerful gaming device, yes, but first and foremost it's a computer small enough to hold in your hand. We've seen how emulators can mimic the operating system of other game consoles (see p.48), so it's not too much of a leap to see how similar techniques can bring the Windows and Linux operating systems to the PSP. But this process isn't easy, or stable – you're running software on hardware that was never intended to be used so radically. Plus, the PSP doesn't have nearly as much processing power and RAM as a full-sized computer, so even if you do manage to get a full-fledged operating system up and running, there's a limit to what you can do with it: you certainly won't be able to run an application like Microsoft Word, or launch any significantly sized programs you may code in Linux.

If you do choose to proceed, it would be helpful, though not absolutely necessary, to familiarize yourself with the Bochs PC emulation project. Bochs is a program that apes the workings of an Intel x86 microchip, and with some modifications Bochs can be made to run on all manner of non-Intel machines (like the PSP). Much like eLoader (see p.56), Bochs establishes an environment inside which you can run other programs or emulators – in this case other operating systems – that normally conform to the standards of an Intel microchip. The Bochs site also has an open library of operating system emulators that can be useful in combination with the **Windows & Linux on the PSP**-specific Bochs emulator mentioned below. And the reverse is also possible. You can emulate the PSP's operating system on a Windows PC, very useful for testing out your backed-up games right on your computer (see p.46).

Frightened of Bochs? Try running a scaled-down version of Windows, and even the Mac OS, using the same method you would for normal homebrew games with Slasher's PSP Windows or the X5 Mac OS emulator.

EXTRAS

141

Bochs http://bochs.sourceforge.net
Windows & Linux on the PSP www.hacker.co.il/psp/bochs
PSP emulator for PCs www.psp-hacks.com/index.php?p=87
Slasher's PSP Windows http://psp-news.dcemu.co.uk/pspwindows.shtml
X5 http://x5.psp3d.com

18

Accessories

protect & modify

At some point you've probably admitted that you love your PSP, so why not prove your love by personalizing and protecting it as you would any other cherished treasure? Beyond giving it a name and sleeping with it under your pillow, there are a variety of PSP accessories available that will show the world (and your PSP) how much you care. While some of these have been born of ergonomic necessity, others are strictly superficial, though considering every PSP comes off the line exactly the same, it's nice to know there are simple changes that can make yours stand out from the crowd. All of the following accessories are available worldwide, and can be purchased through the online vendors listed in the Resources section (see p.193).

GRIPS

Handling the PSP isn't too hard over short periods of time, but keeping hold of the slick surface 40 minutes into Virtua Tennis can be a challenge. Of course, if you don't care how the PSP looks, you could create a similar effect with a few strips of tennis racquet tape and some strategic scuffing, but manufacturers have successfully created PSP grips that offer improved control in an attractive package, and some even provide an additional battery charge that can double your playing time.

Slip-ons

Models include: Pelican, I-nique, Logic3
Cost (approx): $8/£5

143

Do you feel your hands going numb after playing with the PSP for too long? If this condition occurs outside of gaming, see a doctor. Otherwise, get yourself a PSP-cozy like the Flexible Hand Grip. Styled after a PS2 controller, this rubber grip provides a snug fit for the PSP, and its handles are positioned to relieve wrist and finger strain. It also leaves all the buttons and ports exposed, so you'll be as uninhibited as always.

If you want something more streamlined, try a Skin Grip from Pelican or I-nique. These silicone wraps have anti-slip "dimples" and come in a variety of colors to match your mood.

Charger grips

Models include: Satechi, JAVOedge Intl., Vector
Cost (approx): $10–50/£7–30

Battery charger grips are slightly larger and heavier than the slip-on variety, but can carry up to an additional 10 hours of battery life on top of your regular battery. The lightweight Vector model even comes with built-in stereo speakers and a back-mounted fan to keep your circuitry cool and sprightly, and though large on the PSP, it collapses to roughly half its size when not in use, making it easier to jam into an already overstuffed rucksack.

THIRD PARTY ACCESSORIES

For every brand-name peripheral manufacturer, there is an unnamed Hong Kong equivalent making a similar product (sometimes they're even first to the market, and at any given time can make up a large percentage of the PSP accessories available on eBay). But they may not always perform as well as you may have been led to believe – if the unnamed company's offering is drastically cheaper than a similar, branded product, chances are the difference is due in large part to quality. When buying something from an unnamed company, be sure to read reviews of their product online.

CAR MOUNTS

There is a variety of telescopic and pedestal-style mounts available that will create a permanent seat for the PSP in your car – help-

EXTRAS

ful if you want
to use your PSP
as a jukebox or
as an on-board
television dur-
ing road trips.
Most models will
hold the PSP at just

the right angle and distance for
your viewing pleasure, while higher-end options add power cables
and audio connections made specifically to fit your automobile.
You can also purchase audio and power connectors independently. A 5-volt car charger will convert your auto's juice into a
PSP-friendly voltage – try one from eXpansys, Sakar, or Intec for
under $10/£6. And a simple cassette adaptor, like the one pictured
from Belkin ($15/£9), will be sufficient to transfer audio to your
car's stereo system.

Standard mounts

Models include: Arkon
Cost (approx): $30/£20

Basic mounts generally attach to windows (with suction cups) or the bolts
holding your seats to the floor, though
some do come with kits enabling them
to be fixed permanently to the
dashboard. They work by simply
cradling your PSP, while providing a degree of pivot that allows
your neck to remain as motionless
as if you were reclining in a lounge
chair. A device intended specifically

EXTRAS

for passengers, try not to become too distracted by your newest UMD movie while careening around tight mountainous roads, or just rolling up the block for that matter.

Powered mounts

Models include: Arkon, Voyager Ventures
Cost (approx): $70/£45

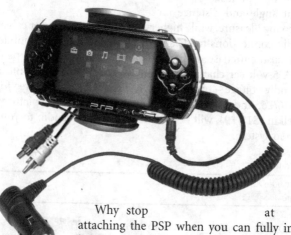

Why stop at simply attaching the PSP when you can fully integrate it into your car's audio system? With the screen playing a movie and the audio pumping through your car's speakers, passengers can enjoy music and movies in full stereo sound (assuming your car has auxiliary audio inputs, see below). These mounts come in standard black but can be found with a steely shine if you're into the futuristic look. And don't worry about the power drain – they include an integrated voltage converter for use with your car's cigarette lighter.

Additional auto options

Models include: eXpansys, Sakar, Intec, Jensen, Griffin
Cost (approx): $10–70/£8–45

These days, most cars are shipped without cassette decks, but the more considerate automobile manufacturers have begun installing factory car stereos with auxiliary audio inputs. If you have a newer car and find yourself in this fortunate position, you can run an audio line from your PSP into the waiting red and white inputs, or 1/8" headphone jack in your car's stereo. If you have an older car and don't want to replace the stereo, you might consider broadcasting your PSP audio to your car's radio using an **FM transmitter**, or you could select a car mount option with built-in speakers, like Arkon's Powered Mount Solution.

Or you can forgo packaged options entirely, add your own auxiliary line to your vehicle's stereo and build your own custom cradle out of anything that will hold the PSP in place. The following sites offer advice and products to help you reconfigure any factory installed automobile stereo:

Installer.com www.installer.com/aux
Car Audio Direct www.caraudiodirect.co.uk
Custom Cradle www.psp411.com/PSP_Car_Mount.html

PERSONALIZING YOUR PSP

When video and computer components were first introduced, they came in shades of beige and gray to match the 1970s decor. Now, with the exception of Apple's styling, they're mostly black or chrome: more attractive, sure, but not very personal. Fortunately you have a few ways to set yourself apart from the crowd.

Skins

Models include: DecalGirl, VinzDecals, Logitech
Cost (approx): $10/£6

Adhesive-backed decals are the quickest and easiest way to change the PSP's overall appearance, and because of their easy on-and-off sticki-ness you can swap them when you're ready for a new look. DecalGirl will even manu-facture a skin of your own design, and provides layout specifications on its PSP skins forum page (see p.194).

Faceplates

Models include: XCM, Project Asterix
Cost (approx): $10–60/£7–40

If you've already downgraded your firmware (see p.115) or played torrented games in an emulator (see p.48), you may be ready for a more invasive means of altering your PSP's appearance – changing the faceplate. There is a variety of colors and different

For the price of a new UMD game you can have Project Asterix's clear faceplate

opacities to choose from, and for the indecisive, there's the option of buying more than one faceplate in a multicolored pack.

Simply remove the 7 screws holding the casing together with a small Phillips screwdriver (like you'd find in an eyeglass kit), and exchange faces. Clear instructions will come in the package, but can also be found at Lik-Sang and DecalGirl (see pp.193-194).

Buttons & analog stick

Models include: NakiWorld, Project Asterix
Cost (approx): $7–15/£5–10

While you've got the faceplate off, you may as well change the buttons to match your PSP's new shell. It's a very simple swap – just be sure not to drop the buttons onto your exposed screen, as any minor abrasion can cause a permanent blur.

On such a streamlined device, the PSP's analog stick fits the overall aesthetic, but a larger node will give you the height and angle needed for better control. Just pop off the original and slide one of these more bulbous knobs back in its place.

PROTECTION

You have plenty of options when it comes to encasing and protecting your PSP, from soft pouches and waterproof bags, to impenetrable containers and foam-lined attaches. And if you're inclined toward higher-end accessories, there are even some designer versions on offer.

Soft cases

Models include: Body Glove, Hori, Core Gamer, XCM, Dunhill, Vaja
Cost (approx): $15–160/£10–100

You do get a soft slip-on pouch when you buy the PSP, but it's not closely fitted, and one entire end is open, making it easy to

This Marc Jacobs offering is high priced but super stylin'.

send the PSP slipping out and onto the floor. Ideally, pouches should give you more protection when you're tossing the PSP into a bag, or if you plan on bringing it kayaking. For the extra-clumsy, there are soft cases that remain attached to your PSP at all times, with cutouts exposing only its buttons, like the high-end Vaja offering.

H3 Hard cases & encasings

Models include: Logitech, Capdase, Intec, CoreCases, Nyko, DragonPlus
Cost (approx): $15–80/£10–50

Prone to fits of imbalanced bumbling? Perhaps you should encase your PSP in an ever-present armored shell. Triggers, buttons, and controllers all poke through, while the rest of the device sits snugly behind thick shock-absorbing plastic; on the downside, the

EXTRAS

The Nyko Theater Experience case protects and serves

extra girth can make control cumbersome unless you also change the analog stick (see p.149).

Other hard cases operate more like eyeglass cases, with a plush interior and a protective outer layer hinged on one side. Some can carry a supplemental charge, so while you protect and transport your PSP its batteries are being rejuvenated. Or, if your intention is to feel like a secret agent, foam-padded attaches are on offer with cut-outs shaped to fit a PSP, UMDs, batteries, and cables.

Screen protectors

Models include: Mad Catz, Intec, Hori, Brando Workshop, Pelican
Cost (approx): $10/£6

There's already a thin plastic layer protecting the PSP's screen, but if that covering gets scratched you'll have to replace the entire faceplate (see p.148). For a little added shielding, lay down a sticky-backed screen protector – before you do, be sure to clean off any dust with a dry shammy.

UMD STORAGE

Models include: Pdair, Nyko, Gamexpert
Cost (approx): $10/£6

There's no need to lug around all your game containers when you have a UMD organizing case. Similar to CD cases, and available in as many varieties, any one of these models will keep your games and memory safe in transit.

DOCKS

Models include: Naki, Logic3, Incipio
Cost (approx): $10-$30/£6-£20

A PSP dock makes it easy to connect and disconnect your PSP to a power source, a computer, and additional speakers. Docks can maintain a dedicated space in your home, meaning connection cables you'd normally have splayed about can find a permanent location hidden from sight. Features are not standard across all the models (while one dock may provide an audio-out jack, another may not), so be sure the manufacturer's listed features meet your needs before you purchase.

Audio docks

Models include: Gamexpert, Logic3, Joytech, Logitech
Cost (approx): $40-60/£20-35

Plugging any powered computer speakers into your PSP will improve the sound, but for a PSP-specific audio enhancer that also recharges your battery, you'll want to invest in an audio dock. Most audio docks are powerful enough to provide clear sound for a decent-sized room, with some providing an array of tweeters and woofers rivaling those in bookshelf stereo systems. Some, like the Logic3 offering, are complete hybrids, providing a charging cradle and a speaker-enhanced grip in one product.

> **TIP** Beware of stands being advertised as "docks." You can set a stand by your bed to watch videos, but it won't recharge your PSP's battery or provide any additional audio capabilities.

BATTERIES & BATTERY PACKS

Models include: Datel, Core Gamer, Logic 3, Brando
Cost (approx): $25-$60/£15-£35

A single charge of the PSP's battery will last a good five hours or so, but hours can seem like minutes when you're searching for that last hidden item, or trying to make it one more game into the playoffs. Before you know it, the green power light starts flashing and you're confronted with a low battery alert. At home, near your charger, this may not be such an issue, but if you're on the road and there's nowhere to top up, you'll need to swap batteries or hook into an external battery pack for a quick boost. External battery packs are especially useful, and the more expensive offerings can hold up to triple the amount of energy of one PSP battery.

There is also a solar-powered battery charger available from Logic3. It can turn just four hours of direct sunlight into enough juice to fully recharge your PSP. And the sun works the same everywhere, so if you travel in different countries frequently you won't need to pack a set of voltage converters.

> **TIP** When buying replacements or extras, look for batteries with a higher
> mAh (milliampere-hours) than the original's 1800 mAh – the higher the
> mAh number, the more energy a battery can hold. Datel, makers of the
> 4GB PSP hard drive (see below), manufacture a battery providing double
> the charge of the original Sony battery, but it is also larger than the original,
> adding about an inch of width onto the back of the PSP as part of an entire
> battery door replacement, so be sure it will fit into your case or pouch
> before you buy.

MEMORY

Memory is one of the biggest issues for the PSP. Rumors have
flown for some time about Sony including an internal hard drive
or some form of solid-state memory (like in fourth generation
iPods) in its next PSP release. But until then you're stuck with
Memory Sticks. However, while Sony suggests that the PSP's
memory slot is for exclusive use with its Memory Stick PRO Duo,
you actually have a number of other options for saving your files,
including adaptors that allow you to swap across a variety of
memory card formats.

Sticks & drives

Models include: Datel, SanDisk, Sony
Cost (approx): $20–280/£13–150

The Value Pack PSP comes packaged with a minuscule 32MB
Memory Stick, and you'll fill that up fast with music, video,
and game saves. But the hardware is designed to handle up to a
37GB Memory Stick – we just need to wait for the firmware and
Memory Stick makers to catch up. Until then, you can reach the
limited heights of 4GB of portable memory using the Datel hard
drive, or a Sony or SanDisk 4GB Memory Stick PRO Duo. At the

time of writing Sony had announced a 8GB offering, but the price had not yet been determined.

Memory adaptors

Models include: Neo, Sony
Cost (approx): $15–80/£10–50

A Memory Stick PRO adaptor comes with some bundled versions of the Sony PRO Duo Memory Stick, and you can use it for backwards compatibility with older Sony devices. But that's not nearly as useful as being able to use other kinds of memory cards with your PSP. There are a handful of formats out there, including Compact Flash (CF) and MMC (Multimedia Card), which don't fit into your PSP. The way to get around this is with an adaptor, and the Japanese company Neo offers 3 solutions: the Neo 2in1, 4in1, and 8in1. The 2in1 can only read Compact Flash and regular PSP Memory Sticks, while the 4in1 adds SuperDisc (SD) and MMC capabilities. Both these versions send a cable to your PSP's memory port while attaching to the UMD door with a circle of Velcro. The third option, the NeoPad 8in1 takes the form of a charger grip (see p.144), providing PS2-style handles and some additional power thanks to its four rechargeable AA batteries.

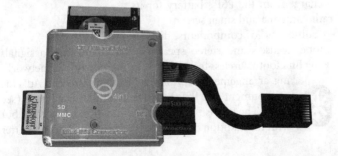

AUDIO ADD-ONS

Models include: Griffin, Bluetake
Cost (approx): $50/£30

You can listen to recorded
audio files on your PSP
using the Memory Stick
(see p.75), or audio streams
with its RSS function (see
p.105), but what about listening to plain old radio? An
integral feature of the first mas-
sively popular portable music
device – the Walkman – with
the now overpowering presence of
radio-less iPods, the airwaves have
been nearly relegated to automobile-
use-only. And even there change is on the
way (see pp.144-147). But if you long for
simpler times, you can listen to regular
radio waves on your PSP with the
Griffin iFM radio tuner. This device
plugs into the headset port, drawing
a charge from the PSP's battery for its
radio antenna and small screen.

Some audio components, like mobile
phone headsets and stereo speakers, can receive audio signals
using Bluetooth wireless technology – an extremely local network-

ing arrangement very similar in design to the Ad Hoc
environment the PSP uses for multiplayer gaming (see
p.93). The PSP isn't Bluetooth compatible on its own, but
with the addition of Bluetake's i-Phono MiNi transmitter

you can send the PSP's audio to wireless Bluetooth headphones or speakers. Like the iFM radio tuner, the i-Phono MiNi plugs into the audio port and powers itself off the PSP battery. And besides the obvious benefit of freeing yourself from the constraints of those asymmetrical headphone cables, Bluetooth devices use entirely accept-able amounts of energy, so you won't lose more than 30 minutes off a maximum battery charge.

A PSP TELEPHONE?

The PSP's USB port suggests a future full of plug-in microphones, cameras, hard drives, you name it – we're just waiting for the PSP's firmware to sup-port this little wonder's potential. Since the summer of 2003, the PSP's big brother, the PlayStation, has accepted an USB video camera that goes by the name **EyeToy**. More than just a way to snap pictures, EyeToy captures your body's movements and uses them to control characters in EyeToy-enabled video games. What's more, it can record and transmit the spoken word using a built-in microphone.

The EyeToy may have cut its chops on the PlayStation, but by the time this book hits the shelves there should be a PSP-compatible version available (and at the very least before the next holiday shopping season). Combined with the PSP's WiFi capabilities, the EyeToy may just be the gateway through which Internet telephony and video transmissions can flow, allowing us audio and video chat capabilities potentially supported in the next big firmware upgrade. In areas that are blanketed in WiFi waves (like San Francisco), could the PSP replace mobile phones?

LOCATION FREE PLAYER – THE ULTIMATE ACCESSORY

If you want to use your PSP to listen to your favorite radio station's online feed, or watch a Web video of Ronaldinho carving his way through a dumbstruck defensive line – you're out of luck. The PSP is simply not advanced enough to handle streaming RealAudio or QuickTime files. But you can enjoy your own music and videos without overloading your Memory Stick, and even watch live TV on-the-fly if you're willing to shell out $300/£175 on the Location Free Player Pak.

Positioned at the center of your media system, the Location Free Player (the Pak part is software for a WiFi-enabled Windows PC) accepts plugs from your stereo, cable box, DVD or VHS player, a PSX hard drive, and either a Digital Video Recorder or TiVo. It can broadcast content from any of these devices over the Internet to your PSP, and also acts as a wireless network antenna around the house.

FIRST AID

△
□
○
✕

19

Help!

troubleshooting & maintenance

The PSP is a miniature computer built for travel – and like with any computer, sometimes things go wrong. The number of problems you can encounter while fiddling around with your PSP appear to be endless, and we just don't have room to go into all of them here. This chapter does, however, cover the most common ailments with suggestions on how you can fix them yourself and at what point you should send your PSP away. We've also included tips for improving your PSP's battery life. And in case nothing here addresses your issue, we've provided links to some helpful online resources.

BASIC FIRST AID

On occasion, maybe when you're on the Web or while you're loading a game save, the PSP will freeze. Your first thought may be that you've bricked your machine, especially if you're running a homebrew program (see p.124). But before you start sobbing like a baby, make sure you haven't just hung it up. The easiest, and most obvious, first step is to turn off the PSP, give it a few seconds so all the energy bleeds from the circuitry, and then turn the PSP back on. Unfortunately, this doesn't always work.

Resetting the PSP

Sometimes when the PSP gets "stuck," simply pushing the power switch in a normal fashion does nothing. Compounding the problem, different applications crash in different ways. Depending on the application you were running at the time of the crash, one of the following tips should help free your PSP from its blank-screened coma.

▸ Pressing **Home** or **Start** will help you escape troublesome UMD games (and hombrew applications running on 1.50 firmware), and bring you back to the main menu.

▸ Holding down the left shoulder button, right shoulder button and Start simultaneously will release you from problematic homebrew running in eLoader.

▸ If the buttons aren't helping, holding the power switch up for 10 seconds will reset the PSP.

▸ If all else fails, you can remove the battery, giving the system about 30 seconds to clear itself before reinserting it.

What is this language?

If you accidentally turn off your PSP during a memory load, or the battery runs out in the middle of game play, you may lose data, and you might also confuse the PSP's operating system into changing its on-screen language. If you can navigate back through the menu in Korean, go right ahead, but if not you can reformat your Memory Stick to reset the operating system language to the standard for the region in which you purchased the PSP – good thing you backed it up already (see p.33).

MEMORY ISSUES

The PSP can be glitchy, and if something goes haywire you may end up unable to reach files you know are on your Memory Stick. Flash memory can wear out over time – a process that happens more quickly when you run homebrew applications, and play movies and music from the Memory Stick, because the constant flow of information moving back and forth between the PSP and the Memory Stick causes extra strain on the circuitry (rather than the minimal usage that occurs during a normal read/write process). If you've backed up your Memory Stick frequently, you'll have your files ready to reload in at least some form of completion. If not, you still have options.

> **TIP** If your PSP isn't seeing files you're certain are on the Memory Stick, connect the PSP to your computer, locate, then move the problem files off the Memory Stick and onto your desktop, and then transfer the files back to the PSP.

Flash memory recovery software

If your Memory Stick files have become corrupted, or you've accidentally deleted the only copy of an important file, you will have to use what's called a flash memory fixer to recover your data. Originally created for digital photo recovery, these programs should be able to resurrect your PSP's data just as well. Each of the following programs is available for download from its respective website, and all of the programs will run on either a Mac or Windows PC (with the exception of the freeware offering).

Media RECOVER ($30) www.mediarecover.com
Photo Rescue ($30/£17) www.datarescue.com/photorescue
ImageRecall (US $30) www.flashfixers.com
ImageRecall (UK £26) www.imagerecall.com
Restoration (freeware) www.snapfiles.com/get/restoration.html

Flash memory retrieval services

Certain data is incredibly valuable, and while we can't imagine a
scenario where the only copy of strategic defense plans would be
housed on a PSP's Memory Stick, some people might lend particularly meaningful pictures equal importance. If your Memory
Stick is completely unresponsive, and you really must have that
data back, consider a send-away option.

Vantage Data Recovery (US) www.vantagetech.com
Southwest Stars Photorescue (US) www.photorescue.com
Cherry Systems (US) www.cherrysystems.com
Data Recovery Doctor (UK) www.datarecoverydoctor.co.uk
Ontrack (UK) www.ontrack.co.uk
Aurora IT Systems (EU) www.aurora.se/flash-memory-cards

SCREEN ISSUES

The PSP's screen is a Liquid Crystal Display (LCD) similar to
those used in flat-screen monitors or laptops. It's made up of
thousands of pixels, each capable of turning off or on, or display-
ing one of three colors: red, green, or blue. Combining these three
colors gives the impression of a color palette of millions, but if
pixels start misfiring, the onscreen image can be impaired. If you
notice that certain little rectangles of color are always dark, or
always one color, you've got a pixel problem.

Checking for stuck pixels

Each pixel on the LCD screen channels a small electric current telling it what color it should turn. Sometimes, pixels can become overwhelmed and get "stuck" on one color at all times. But you may be able to shock them back into working by running a stuck pixel fixer. Nothing more than a video rapidly flashing through the LCD color spectrum, the fixer means to create enough chaos that stuck pixels will be forced to let go of their stubborn charge. You'll have to install it onto your Memory Stick in the video folder as described in the section on p.71.

Nickwiz14's stuck pixel fixer **www.psp-vault.com/Article168.psp**

Always-dark pixels are, unfortunately, dead. Depending on the number and location of your dead pixels, and provided you've done nothing to void your warranty, Sony may fix it for you.

165

North America customer service **1-800/345-7669**
UK customer service **08705/998877**
Ireland customer service **0818/365065**

Replacing the screen

LCD screens are susceptible to extreme temperatures, strong magnetic fields, and, of course, gravity. If your screen breaks, warps, or is otherwise damaged and you have no one to blame but yourself, you'll have to replace it. There are companies that will perform the service for you, but if you're at all mechanically inclined and want to save on the cost of shipping and labor, you can buy a new screen and install it yourself with relative ease. Turn

Never fear – instructions are included.

to the Resources section for a list of parts and repair options (see p.194).

1. Open the faceplate and release the latches on the sides of the screen (see p.149).

2. Flip the screen over to reveal its connection to the PSP motherboard.

3. With a small screwdriver, flip all the latches securing the connection.

4. Remove the damaged LCD screen and connect the new one.

5. Position the new screen, attach the side latches, and replace the faceplate.

> **TIP** For broken casings, cracked buttons, or shredded analog sticks, head to the Accessories section (p.142), where you'll find a wide variety of replacement and enhancement options for the PSP.

BATTERY MAINTENANCE

Everything eventually dies, and the PSP's lithium ion battery is not the exception that proves the rule. It will take about 500 full charges before you have to replace it, though you'll notice it can hold less and less energy as you approach that limit. Here are some ways to milk it for all it's worth.

Extending a single charge

▸ The screen uses a significant portion of your energy – shorten the amount of time before the backlight goes dark. You'll find this option under **Power Save Settings ▸ Backlight Auto-Off.**

A number of helpful battery
life options can be found in
the Power Save Settings.

▸ Also under Power
Save Settings, set a
shorter **Auto Sleep**
time. This turns off the WiFi card, the UMD reading laser, and
all other non-essential internal operations.

▸ Turn off **Key Tones** under **Sound Settings**.

▸ Use lower-quality audio and video file formats (see pp.63,75)
so that the PSP won't have to work as hard playing them.

▸ Use the hold button to avoid turning on the machine and
draining its life by accident.

Extending battery life

▸ Charge the battery as often as you can, but about once a month
let it run down completely before recharging it.

▸ Avoid exposing the PSP and its battery to extreme
temperatures.

If through some unfortunate twist of fate your battery up and
dies on you, you can find a number of replacements (some with
significant advantages over the original) in the Accessories section
(see p.153).

> **TIP** Even if you've bricked your PSP, its parts still hold some value. Your
> screen, some circuitry, and the casing and buttons can all be sold (in parts
> or as a whole) to PSP repair services (see p.194) or to individuals over auc-
> tion sites like eBay.

20

Network issues

when all else fails

Network connection problems are some of the most frustrating you can encounter. PSP online games will only run properly over a high-speed Internet connection, and depending on the requirements of your Internet Service Provider (ISP) and your wireless router, you may be unable to use the easy setup explained in the Networking chapter (see p.91). Following is some basic advice to help you make a finicky wireless network accept your PSP, and a few tips on where to find your local network and router information. If you have a network problem you're still unable to resolve after reading this chapter, check the Resources section (p.177) for a list of technology forums where you can ask a community of Web-heads for suggestions.

Basic networking advice

▶ Turn on the WLAN switch – it's like losing your glasses only to discover them on your head.

▶ Up the power – under Power Save Settings, turn off the WLAN Power Save option.

▶ Avoid areas with lots of wireless networks transmitting information over the airwaves – cordless phones, Bluetooth devices, even insect zappers and fluorescent lights send off a frequency that could potentially interfere with your wireless signal.

▶ Don't sit too far away from the wireless point you're trying to reach, and don't situate yourself so too many walls are between you.

Ad Hoc help

If you get interference when playing multiplayer Ad Hoc games, ensure that:

▶ All PSP systems are using the same channel, and other wireless devices in the area (like your wireless router) aren't using that channel.

▶ All of the PSPs that are trying to connect together are within the range of the PSP hosting the game (no more than 20ft away).

Infrastructure help

If the PSP's Easy network setup works you'll be online in minutes, otherwise you may very well find yourself lost in the nightmare-ish world of port forwarding, MAC filtering, and dedicated IP addresses. But before you go digging into your wireless router settings and calling your Internet Service Provider, check to see if any of the following basic fixes works out the bug.

▶ Test to see if your wireless network is actually working by attempting a connection with a laptop or other wireless-enabled computer.

▸ Are you using an 802.11g wireless router? The PSP only operates the 802.11b protocol, so you'll have to set your router to accept communications accordingly.

▸ If you're certain all your network settings are correct and the network continually refuses you access, try unplugging your modem and router, wait 10 seconds, then plug them back in. The next time you attempt a PSP connection your network should accept it.

Wireless router help

If all else fails, you can try entering your wireless network information manually using the fields available during Custom Network Settings (see p.96). To find this information, you'll need to access your wireless router management screen. The startup disc or instruction manual that came with your router should provide you with an IP address that will bring you to your router's management screen (it may also be printed right on the device, near the bar code). Make a note of your Local Area Network (LAN) settings and your router settings, then transfer the information into the appropriate fields using the PSP's Custom Network setup.

Try one of the following for more detailed information on wireless routers:

PSP 411 www.psp411.com/show/guide/30
EZLAN.NET www.ezlan.net
WiFi 411 www.wifi411.com
Port Forward www.portforward.com/routers.htm

RESOURCES

△
□
○
✕

21

Resources

websites & services

While we've included online resources within each chapter of this book, there are so many websites dedicated to so many different PSP topics, it seems reasonable to provide a list of some of the better ones. The following resources will keep you up-to-date on the latest PSP developments, help you cheat your way through difficult games, and introduce you to forums where you can directly interact with the PSP community. You'll also find links to maintenance sites, and a list of the better video game periodicals on offer.

NEWS & DISCUSSION

PSP news

The official PSP website
www.yourpsp.com

Optimized for your PSP's Internet Browser, and ripe with game, video, and audio downloads, this site will keep you up-to-date with all things Sony.

PSP Fanboy
www.pspfanboy.com

Unabashedly in love with the PSP, this community of bloggers and contributors freely exhibit emotions normally reserved for scantily dressed manga characters.

PSP World
www.pspworld.com

From the handlers of PS3 Informer, this well maintained and extensive site is a great place to scope out accessories, check game reviews, and uncover cheat codes.

Sony PSP Info
www.sonypspinfo.com

Although always chock full of up-to-the-minute info and containing an exhaustive links section, the games arcade is by far the site's best feature – you can download games to your PSP, or play straight from your Web browser using firmware version 2.70.

PSP Drive
www.pspdrive.com

PSP news, of course, but also loads of saved games, photo-based downloadable magazines, links to free audio content, homebrew freeware, and an extensive list of RSS channels for those of you sporting 2.60 firmware (and higher).

Xtreme PSP
www.xtremepsp.com

This PSP-optimized Web site is always running a timewasting survey or two, and its FAQ section offers solutions to many of the most common firmware problems you may encounter.

PSPrimed
www.psprimed.com

Don't be turned off by the tightly layered script and hard-to-read shades of gray, this is a great catch-all site that aggregates the latest news from gaming industry channels.

PSP Culture
www.pspculture.co.uk

A religiously updated blog intent on feeding the obsessive nature of PSP owners.

Kotaku
www.kotaku.com/gaming/psp

A full editorial staff provides breaking news on homebrew and add-ons, while including interesting tidbits on the PSP's influence on our culture at large.

Qj.net
http://pspupdates.qj.net

Its main portal dedicated to online video game journals for all the consoles, the PSP portion is obsessively updated with hombrew releases, third-party product launches, and recaps of Sony press releases.

Gadget news

PSP Gadgetry
www.pspgadgetry.com

Though slightly less frequently updated than the other gadget sites listed here, PSP Gadgetry has the advantage of not over-whelming the reader with a poorly designed layout and loads of flashing adverts.

Engadget
www.engadget.com

Breaking news on iPods, robotics, video blogs (vlogs), political agendas, and the PSP, all rolled into one massive site cross-linked across news services and blogs focused on the intersection of culture and technology.

Gizmodo
www.gizmodo.com

If you like shiny new toys then this is the site for you. Unreleased products always seem to make their way to these pages before they get anywhere else, and the turnaround time between receipt and report is simply astounding.

Ubergizmo
www.ubergizmo.com

A product alert blog and price comparison tool in one, Ubergizmo not only reveals breaking trends, it tells you where to buy the

products that will make your friends green with envy. The site also offers a French language version, perfect for boning up on irregular verbs before your next mid-term exam.

The Gadgeteer
www.the-gadgeteer.com

News on cameras, laptops, and handhelds (along with the occasional glue-gun post) from your hosts Julie and Judie. A spotlight feature on interesting real-life gadgeteers makes this one of the more interactive gadget sites out there – if you manage a DIY video hood for your PSP (see p.138), this is the place to report your triumph.

8BitJoystick
www.8bitjoystick.com

8BitJoystick.com
E-ZINE FOR NERDS

Nostalgia at its finest, this site's name harks back to the days of the original Nintendo, though its content pushes beyond – well beyond. Of note are posts on those tabletop games almost exclusively found in retro-style pubs, videogame to movie cross-overs, and rants about beans.

Help & forums

Ask Dave Taylor
www.askdavetaylor.com

Dave Taylor seems to have answers for every sort of technological problem you might encounter, from computers and networking, to mobile phones and the PSP. Check the well-organized archives before pressing the giant red "Contact Dave" button, though Dave will direct you to the right place if you leap before looking.

PSP 411
www.psp411.com/list/forum

PSP chatter is the rule of the land, though there are a few threads delving into the next generation of consoles, mostly taking the form of PS3 versus Wii debates.

PSP Forums
www.pspforums.com/forums

Nearly 10,000 users populate these threads with tips, tricks, game saves, and advice on hacks, mods, and cheats. For your basic questions, check out the comprehensive beginners guides in "n00b central" – be warned that moronic questions are met with disdain.

PlayStation Forums
boardsus.playstation.com/playstation?category.id=top

The official board maintained by Sony, this site houses all manner of PlayStation information for all the manufacturer's consoles, including plenty of discussions on hacks and firmware work-arounds, and a handy section on wireless networking with the PSP.

DCEmu
www.dcemu.co.uk/vbulletin

With a home page full of homebrew, and a forum covering nearly every videogame console since the jump to 32-bit processors, DCEmu is a all-in-one resource for pretty much any questions you might have.

Sengo Forums
www.sengo.com/forums

One of the friendlier videogame forums, due in no small part to its moderators' calming influence in the face of flaming arguments.

Magazines

179

Edge
(monthly; £4)

Geared toward an audience who laugh at regional encoding while ordering Japanese releases of games months before they hit the English-speaking market, *Edge* provides previews, interviews, developer profiles, and in-depth games reviews across all consoles.

Electronic Gaming Monthly
(monthly; $4.99)

A long-running 'zine with a format often imitated, but never duplicated. EGM generally dedicates it's cover story to a major game release, complete with exclusive screen captures, preliminary walk-throughs and tricks, all delivered with a twist of wit.

Play
(monthly; $5.99)

Merging the teen obsessions of gaming and anime, *Play* embraces "that very special and rare connection between game and player."

Game Informer
(monthly; $4.99)

Since the early 90s *Game Informer* has reported on the world of console and PC games, providing strategy guides and cheats along the way. An excellent read on the whole, though a certain staff member seems a bit too into Jigglypuff.

games™
(monthly; £4)

games^tm explores the history and culture of videogames while analyzing the current trends and blockbuster releases – all within a design so well-crafted it may occasionally gloss your eye with a joyful tear.

Heroes & Villains
(bi-monthly; $5.99)

Some people like sports games, others like shooters, but if you're obsessed with superhero and fantasy cross-overs then this recently launched magazine is the one for you. Learn how to create your own JLA team, find out the top ten heroes of all time, and price your action figure collection with their handy collectors section.

Official U.S. PlayStation Magazine
(monthly; $8.99)

From the mothership itself, this high-priced offering always comes with a CD full of demos, and is certainly a great resource – if you're only interested in Sony devices.

Official UK PlayStation Magazine
(monthly; £4.99)

Touted as the "the best-selling PlayStation publication in the world" this magazine and its US counterpart are essentially the same, except for the games on which they choose to focus – two nations separated by a common language, indeed.

SOFTWARE, HOMEBREW, HACKS, & MODS
Audio decryption

31 Tunebite
www.tunebite.com

Transform your purchased audio files into a format the PSP understands with Tunebite, an audio converter that let's you crack the copy-protection on WMA, AAC, and MP4 files so you can play them on finicky computers, iPods, and your PSP.

Hymn Project
www.hymn-project.org

Information wants to be free – break open the audio encryption on your iTunes music files so that you can play them with any music software on any capable device.

Audio Hijack pro
www.rogueamoeba.com

Beyond removing that pesky encryption, Audio Hijack provides a palette of audio editing and recording options, with effects added to boot. Elsewhere on Rogue Amoeba's site you can find programs that help you set up your own Internet radio station, and transmit RealPlayer and QuickTime audio content wirelessly to your stereo.

Homebrew

QuickJump Downloads
http://dl.qj.net/PSP/catid/106

Though not much more than a massive server housing most of the stand-alone homebrew programs you'll ever need, without QJ, the propagation of PSP firmware enhancements might just come along as slowly as a Windows release.

1Homebrew
www.1homebrew.com/psp/psp.shtml

It's not pretty, but it's got what you want. Check out the category box on the home page for a directory by type, and the madly updated news links for a more random spattering of current releases.

Noobz (Fanjita)
http://noobz.eu

Hands-down, the best there is.

Lua Player
www.luaplayer.org

Homebrew can sometimes act like a red-haired cousin, but when original software is created in Lua it tends to run a touch more smoothly.

Bochs
http://bochs.sourceforge.net

The original x86 Intel chip emulator, Bochs is not for n00bs.

Emulators & game ROMs

Emuparadise
www.emuparadise.org

Chock full of emulators and homebrew applications, this is the place to come when you have a yearning to play Donkey Kong on your PSP.

PSP ROMs
www.psproms.info

Cheats and codes, and ROM downloads, and little lambs eat ivy.

Euro Emu
www.euroemu.net/home.php

183

Annoying pop-ups aside, this site boasts a massive catalog of ROMs, and all the emulators to play them. If for some reason you can't find what you're looking for, check out the list of affiliates for thirty or so other online libraries.

ROMs Central
www.romscentral.com

Optimized for FireFox fans, this ROM warehouse forces you to vote for it at 5 different ROM ranking sites before letting you get to the goods. Is it worth the effort? Well, we counted over 5000 ROMs available for download, so the answer is an emphatic yes.

PSP News

http://psp-news.dcemu.co.uk

Primarily a news site, PSP News also hosts a large library of emulators, homebrew games, UMD loaders and downgraders, as well as a lengthy list of the hottest new import games available from lik-sang (see p.193).

PSP-Hacks

www.psp-hacks.com/category/13

Game saves and backgrounds are up for grabs on this massive site, but you won't find a better place for the latest homebrew and emulator developments, all downloadable directly.

Hacks & mods

hack a day

www.hackaday.com

This site sets its focus well beyond the PSP, but there are still quite a few PSP hacks here. Each day blog master Eliot Phillips chooses the best hardware hack on the Web, and describes how to do it with both text and pictures.

PSP Hacks
www.psphacks.net

A cornucopia of homebrew applications, hardware hacks, breaking news, and helpful forums. Click on the blog link for a PSP-optimized page without images – an easy way to avoid that hated "out of memory" Internet Browser error.

PSPmod
www.pspmod.com

A specialized forum for the do-it-yourselfer, this site contains threads on hardware and software modifications, with additional content on homebrew and media file manipulation.

MakeZine
www.makezine.com/blog/archive/psp

Looking for a Lego docking station or a PSP controlled helicopter? Look no further. MakeZine brings together some of the weirdest PSP inspired creations we've seen, and encourages you to go forth and create similar efforts of your own.

Media managers

iPSP
http://ipsp.kaisakura.com/ipsp.php

Mimicking the iTunes interface, iPSP backs up your games, manages your music, converts video, and transfers bookmarks between your computer and PSP. The free version is useful, but you'll need to invest in the full version for video conversions longer than 10 minutes.

PSP Media Manager
www.sonymediasoftware.com

From the house that Ibuka built comes a simple drag-and-drop media manager. Our only criticism – if iTunes is free, why isn't this?

PSPWare
www.nullriver.com

PSPWare will let you listen to your iTunes music library wirelessly, and its Sync Profiles feature is smart enough to not overwrite data on different Memory Sticks.

PSPWare
The PSP Media Companion

Torrent sites

IsoHunt
http://isohunt.com

ISOHUNT Hunting for ISOs? Here you go. This site is most useful if you already know what you're looking for, but search for "PSP" and you'll come across numerous copies of UMD games.

Mininova
www.mininova.org

A torrent site with decent subcategories – if you're not sure what you're looking for, or want to just see what's out there, mininova is a good place to browse.

mininova

The Pirate Bay
http://thepiratebay.org

A safe haven for pirates? Perhaps. But it will also point you to legitimate (and illegitimate) programs and software for the PSP.

Torrent Reactor
www.torrentreactor.net

A rather good selection of torrents, but not for kids, or anyone who might find R- to X-rated banner ads objectionable.

Wallpaper

deviantART
http://handhelds.deviantart.com/pspwallpaper

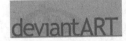

All sorts of user-created images to use as PSP wallpaper, from photos to modified band logos to crazy reptile eyes. Fearsome.

My PSP
www.mypsp.com.au/wallpaper.aspx

A few thousand more backgrounds for your PSP, mostly of video games, movies, and TV shows, and a whole section dedicated to the actress Jessica Alba.

Plasma Design
www.plasmadesign.co.uk/PSP.htm

A handful of mostly hand-created PSP backgrounds to download.

PSP Wallpapers
www.pspwallpapers.com

Backgrounds for your PSP; heavy on models and adult content, although they have everything from celebrity photos to basic patterns, too.

Space Wallpaper
www.spacewallpapers.net/psp-wallpaper/

Fractals and space images for the aliens among us.

ThemePSP
www.themepsp.com

Every variety of PSP wallpaper, organized by theme, from animals to weather via movies, manga, and males.

ThePSPimp
http://thepspimp.com

Thousands of wallpapers to trick out your PSP.

MEDIA DOWNLOADS

Sony media downloads

PSP Connect
http://psp.connect.com

Some PSP-specific content from Sony – mostly game trailers and promotional items from their content partners like the auto website edmunds.com.

Sony Connect Music Store
http://musicstore.connect.com

Sony Connect Europe
www.connect-europe.com

Sony's online music store – not a bad alternative to iTunes, but it's exclusively for Windows and Sony devices.

GAMES

Game news & cheats

CheatCodes
http://cheatcodes.com/psp

The name says it all.

GamePro
www.gamepro.com

Reviews, cheats, features, and more – like pretty good writing, which is something of a rarity in the gaming press.

GameSkanker
www.gameskanker.com

Comprehensive site featuring cheats and walkthroughs for a vast array of games. Some do turn out to be external links, but it's a thorough site nonetheless.

GameSpot
www.gamespot.com

Like Old Faithful, CNET's GameSpot always delivers. One of the most comprehensive and knowledgeable gaming news sites on the web. Highly recommended.

GamesTracker
http://uk.gamestracker.com/psp

Frequent updates on new game releases for the UK market.

GameZone
http://psp.gamezone.com/hints/hints.htm

Lots of links to quality cheats for PSP games.

Joystiq
www.joystiq.com

All sorts of gaming news, plus discussion of gaming and other electronic culture. Visit to get a handle on where the anti-gaming lobby is at in its ongoing battle against, well, everybody.

The Magic Box
www.the-magicbox.com

  News and rumours on what's coming out when, how many people think the PS3 is priced too high

(hint: everybody), and so forth. A good place to visit if you need to feel smarter than your gaming peers.

WorthPlaying
www.worthplaying.com

A blog-like, gossipy site about pretty much everything gaming. A second home for obsessives – just check out the posting times of content manager Rainier Van Autrijve, who seems to never sleep.

Game rentals & purchasing

Boomerang
www.boomerangrentals.co.uk

Monthly fee: £7.99–15.99
Smallish selection, but a bit cheaper than its UK rivals.

GameFly
www.gamefly.com

Monthly fee: $14.95–35.95
One of the pioneering online game rental sites in the US, with a comprehensive selection of UMD games and movies. You can save up to $30 per game by purchasing from the used section.

Gamelender
www.gamelender.com

Monthly fee: $19.99–34.99
Thousands of US games for rent, from the most recent UMD releases all the way back to games like 10 Yard Fight for the original NES.

Play.com
www.play.com

The UK's huge online media store offers a typically broad selection of new UMD games and movies. ▶ PLAY.COM

SwapGame
www.swapgame.co.uk

Monthly fee: £9.99–19.99
Games for all currently available major systems, accompanied by member ratings to help you decide. Used UMDs are for sale as well, to keep a few extra quid in your pocket.

Game saves

PSP Cheats
www.psp-cheats.org

With the tagline, "It's not cheating. It's helping," this site's game saves are handily sorted into Japanese, American, and European sections.

PSP Game Saves
www.pspgamesaves.com

Registration is required to leap ahead in your games without having to do the work.

PSP-Saves
www.psp-saves.net

More and more saves. Doesn't anybody play games all the way through anymore?

PSP Saves
http://pspsaves.info

Ditto.

PSP Vault
www.psp-vault.com/UpDownload.psp

A few hundred game saves, sorted by game title and region, so you can get saves for Japanese, European, or American games.

HARDWARE

Accessories

Gold International Trading Co.
http://e-linksoft.com

"Sunny Yellow" PSP faceplates, Chrome Xbox controllers, and the kitchen sink.

Kelkoo
www.kelkoo.co.uk

Owned by Yahoo!, Kelkoo's site has much the same functionality. Limited selection of accessories.

Lik-Sang
http://lik-sang.com

A Hong Kong-based seller of all things video games. Order everything from the ceramic white PSP to Japan-only games to adapters that let you use other forms of memory with the PSP. One of the most comprehensive gaming-related retailers we've encountered.

Neo Flash
www.neoflash.com

The maker of the Neo-PSP 4-in-1 Pad, which gives your PSP more memory options and extra batteries.

PSP World
www.pspworld.co.uk

Extensive selection of basic PSP accessories, from Memory Sticks to skins to speaker mounts.

Parts & maintenance

Fix My Playstation (US)
www.fixmyplaystation.com

PS2 and PSP repairs. Offers LCD, laser, and Power Switch replacements for the PSP

GT Electronics (UK)
www.gtelectronics.co.uk

Scottish repair shop offering competitive prices and a six-month warranty. No parts for sale.

Llamma (US)
www.llamma.com/PSP

Lots of mods, replacement parts, and tutorials on fixing your PSP. They also offer a reasonably priced replacement service that includes the cost of one major part.

New Age Console Service (US)
www.newagepsx.com

Repair for all game machines. New Age sells parts and also offers the same replacement services as Fix My Playstation, but at slightly cheaper prices.

Portable Repair (US)
www.portablerepair.com

Service for your PSP, with warranty.

PSP Repair (UK)
www.psprepair.co.uk

Undertakes common repairs, and provides a 180-day warranty on work. You can also order PSP replacement parts from the site.

PSP Tree (UK)
www.psptree.co.uk

Comprehensive selection of parts and accessories for the PSP. A great place to go if you have the technical skills to repair your own machine.

PSX Repair (US/UK)
www.psxrepair.com

Parts and services for PSP, PS2, PSOne, and Xbox.

INDEX

△
□
○
✕

21

Index

SYMBOLS

A

N

O

Q

R

S